Supplier Negotiation Made Simple

Daniel Gérard

Supplier Negotiation Made Simple

The 4C Method

Compose – Clarify
Confront – Commit

Foreword by Ed Ainsworth

de boeck

For further information about our catalogue and new titles in your field,
visit our website: **www.deboeck.com**

1th edition

Fond Jean Pâques, 4 – 1348 Louvain-la-Neuve

Printed in Belgium

National Library, Paris: august 2014
Royal Belgian Library, Brussels: 2014/0074/240

ISSN 1373-0274
ISBN 978-2-8041-8921-1

Foreword

Developing a profitable growth model in an uncertain economic climate is an exciting challenge businesses are facing today. Despite unprecedented financial and market conditions, a number of European businesses are successful even in the most difficult times and they forge paths for others to follow.

Traditionally, businesses were cutting costs in economic downturns and growing sales in upturns. Today, successful businesses have shifted from defensive cost-cutting to cultural cost awareness, as a way to auto-finance growth, while many investors still shy from risks and cut equity exposure.

Buying quality goods and services at the best competitive price rather than the price they are ready to pay is a way for them to unlock their capacity to finance other profitable growth initiatives.

Supplier Negotiation Made Simple has helped a number of our clients in reaching this ambitious objective. I am therefore delighted to introduce you to the 4C method so you too can obtain *"more for less"* from your suppliers so as to support profitable growth in your interest – which in the end is theirs also.

Ed Ainsworth
Managing Director
4C Associates

Table of contents

Part 2
NEGOTIATION PROCESS

Part 3
NEGOTIATING TECHNIQUES

Part 4
THE 4C METHOD

Part 5
CASE STUDY

Part 1

INTRODUCTION TO NEGOTIATIONS

Chapter 1

Negotiations and you

Every individual negotiates according to how they perceive the meaning of negotiations. For example, depending upon whether they view negotiating as a sport or as a combat, they adopt the behaviour they consider to be the most appropriate, an instinctively different way of doing things. Yes, but... what if they are mistaken about their perception of negotiation? What about you? Are you sure you have not got a misconceived idea about negotiating and have you ever assessed your results?

1.1 THE NEGOTIATION QUIZ

The following quiz has no scientific nor any other pretensions. It has the sole purpose of making you respond, in one way or another to a series of considerations directly related to the negotiation process and then, to reflect upon your answers.

The quiz is ultra simple. Read each statement and answer instinctively to each one, with either "agree" or "disagree".

Do not ponder over your answers, let your instinct take the lead. This is not about testing you but about testing your instincts.

Then mark your answers to determine whether your approach towards negotiations is instinctive approach or rational.

Are you ready?

Read the following quiz and answer the questions taking no more than 3 seconds between finishing reading the question and marking the "Agree" or "Disagree" column.

	STATEMENT	AGREE	DISAGREE
1.	Negotiating is a question of instinct, culture and personality and is something that cannot be learned.		
2.	To negotiate well, the other party should not be allowed too much time to express their own arguments.		
3.	In negotiations, the best form of defence is attack. To start the negotiations is to start the battle of wits.		
4.	Negotiating is a waste of time. It is better to clearly set out what you want, and let the other party take it or leave it.		
5.	You have to assert yourself at the start of a negotiation, define your position, defend it and not be swayed in any way.		
6.	A friendly approach in a negotiation is to cover up an underlying fear that your positions will not please the other party.		
7.	In negotiations you have to avoid tension, rationale must prevail over emotions.		
8.	The ideal situation is to dominate the other party to a degree that you control the negotiation and its outcome.		
9.	In order to negotiate for your best interests, you have to use the "carrot and the stick" concept.		
10.	Commercial negotiations must be rational and objective, there is no room for acting.		
11.	Good negotiators know how to change course according to the circumstances.		
12.	You have to have the ability not to compromise as to compromise is to lose ground.		
13.	To negotiate is to lose your free will and to a large extent concede to the diktat of the other party.		
14.	In any event, negotiating always comes down to meeting each other halfway.		
15.	In a negotiation, each party has to gain as much as the other.		
16.	The opposite of negotiating is collaborating. If you collaborate well, it is no longer necessary to negotiate.		
17.	It is never possible to find a solution that pleases everybody.		
18.	Negotiating is a contest in which one of the parties loses, the question is "how much"?		
19.	To ask for too much in a negotiation is neither moral nor ethical vis-à-vis the other party.		

	STATEMENT	AGREE	DISAGREE
20.	Negotiating is a serious business, it is definitely not a game.		
21.	Negotiating is to reach a compromise. It is to lose the difference between what you wanted to obtain at the beginning and what you actually achieved.		
22.	Negotiating is a trial of strength, power or authority that enables you to achieve what you want.		
23.	The most effective negotiation is one in which you are able to skilfully and subtly trick the other party in such a manner that they do not even notice.		
24.	A good negotiator maintains his views and never sways.		
25.	Negotiating is to accept that you will finally end up with something that you did not want as there is no other alternative.		
26.	Negotiating is daring to say "no" more often than "yes" to the other party.		
27.	To negotiate well essentially means taking your time in order to analyse before deciding.		
28.	You should never consult the other party regarding your position, with a future negotiation in mind, as this would reveal your strategy.		
29.	Telling tales during negotiations always destroys the climate of trust.		
30.	If you have to negotiate, it means that you have neither the power nor the authority necessary to assert yourself.		

1.2 THE RESULTS OF THE QUIZ

The 30 questions that you have just answered are all preconceived ideas about negotiations that prevent us from negotiating objectively.

For the most part, these are unfounded beliefs that live within the western society as, we have to confess, the majority of us do not like to negotiate and more often than not, are scared to do so.

The results of the quiz are thus child's play. The correct answer to every statement is "DISAGREE".

- Less than 15 "disagrees": You have done well to get this book, as you need to review your ideas about negotiations.
- From 15 to 20 "disagrees": You are on the right track but you have to persevere. This book should help you to, and also provide you with negotiating techniques.
- From 20 to 25 "disagrees": Do not change anything, you are ready to expand your negotiating techniques and become a master in the art.
- More than 25 "disagrees": Either you have done this quiz before, or you are already a negotiating specialist, or, you are quite simply gifted and this book should teach you why.

Chapter 2

Negotiation profiles

When acting on impulse, every negotiator will have a natural tendency towards a stereotypical behaviour called negotiation profile. This will depend upon their personality and approach towards negotiating, nevertheless, their behaviour will strongly influence the negotiation, but not necessarily in the right direction. It is thus essential to understand the implications each behaviour type will have on the other party. This enables anticipation of their reactions, be it natural behaviour or to elicit certain reactions by intentionally adopting a specific behaviour.

2.1 AGGRESSIVE PROFILE VERSUS FRIENDLY PROFILE

The first type of profile is centred on the quality (or lack of it) of the relationship that is established with the other party. At one extreme is the aggressive profile and at the other is the friendly profile.

The aggressive negotiator looks for a win-lose result through a conflicting relationship. He can only concede to having won his negotiation if the other party has lost.

Typical behaviour of an aggressive negotiator:

- Constant criticism in order to place themselves in a strong position, thereby positioning the other party in a weak position.
- The use of proverbs and sayings as arguments and expressing opinions in the form of universal truths.
- They neither ask nor propose, but demand and threaten retaliation if they do not obtain what they want.
- They consider the best form of defence is attack and strike at every opportunity.
- They alternate between the carrot and the stick concept, flattery when the other party agrees and intimidation when they do not.

Inexperienced negotiators often wrongly believe that aggressive behaviour is an effective means of conducting a negotiation. In fact, it is risky as it instils a sense of defeat in the other party and a desire for revenge at the first opportunity. It is also a short-term approach as further negotiations with the same person will become very difficult. In general, an aggressive negotiator rapidly "burns out" and soon learns that they are unable to negotiate again with those who are aware of their reputation.

On the other hand, the friendly negotiator seeks to establish a climate of trust with the other person through a certain social proximity and complicity:

- They are warm and considerate. Their favourite weapon is emotion and have no hesitation to move away from the professional domain and make incursions into the private domain.
- In the event of disagreement, criticism or conflict, they rapidly attempt to smooth over tensions and to defuse the situation.
- They prefer to aim for partnerships and durable relationships.
- Consciously or otherwise, they very often look for a compromise as the outcome of a negotiation.

Negotiators who are reluctant to truly negotiate are quick to adopt a friendly behaviour. In the latter case, it is more of an evasion, although friendly behaviour does not per se exclude the possibility to negotiate, even firmly, and influences the climate and fosters a long term relationship.

The balance is always between these two extreme profiles as they are often used to prompt a given reaction from the other party. Aggressive behaviour may be used intentionally at the start of a negotiation to put pressure on the opposing negotiator, to unsettle them, to put them in a position of inferiority. Programmed friendly behaviour is regularly used, as the negotiation moves forward in the desired direction in order to encourage the other person to continue on this course.

2.2 DOMINATING PROFILE VERSUS SUBMISSIVE PROFILE

The second type of behaviour is centred on the balance (or lack of it) of the opposing forces. At one extreme is the dominating profile and at the other is the submissive profile.

The dominating negotiator deliberately seeks to establish an imbalanced relationship in their favour but do not necessarily resort to aggression. They can appear very friendly, but in such a case are not spontaneous and are in fact applying a strategy. Their objective is to dominate the talks in order to direct the negotiation to their advantage.

A dominating negotiator is very quickly recognised:

- They have a strong personality with an intelligence well above average or an impressive stature.
- They either have substantial power, enabling them to decide single-handedly as to the importance of an issue, or show great authority that allows them to easily get people to adopt their ideas.

— They use their expertise, position, vocabulary, and above all their richness of argument.
— They use body and non-verbal language more than the average person.

The dominating negotiators regard themselves as born winners, however, in contrast to the aggressive negotiators, their victory alone will suffice as their initial goal is not necessarily to defeat the other party.

On the other hand, the submissive negotiator is quite the opposite, a loser by nature with an attitude in negotiations which is above all, a form of eluding confrontation with the other person and fleeing the situation:

— They generally lack confidence or preparation, rarely express what they should state, even if relevant.
— They have a passive attitude, can even go unnoticed and have difficulty expressing themselves clearly.
— They allow themselves to be mistreated, even ridiculed, and reach their limitations when confronted by an aggressive negotiator irritated by their passive attitude.
— They have a tendency to think negatively, to inspire pity, and rapidly show resignation and frustration.

Submissive negotiators are thereby forced to change their approach towards negotiations or to step down and leave others to negotiate in their place.

The best attitude is to display a slightly dominating behaviour, to better control or conduct the negotiation through strategic accelerations at key moments, without crushing the other party.

2.3 ANALYTICAL PROFILE VERSUS INTUITIVE PROFILE

The third type of behaviour is centred on the decision mechanism. At one extreme is analytical profile and at the other is the intuitive profile.

Analytical negotiators follow a sequential and progressive process which leads them to analyse the decision:

— They proceed sequentially by analysis, hypothesis and argument.
— They follow a progression of successive rational thought (each element one after the other).
— They collect and analyse the information, organise it into a hierarchy, and then proceed with deduction and conclusion.
— Their decision is reputed to be "objective".

Analytical behaviour is very typical of the western world. Just imagine an engineer or an accountant conducting a negotiation; reasoning and figures become an effective tool for them.

The reaction of the intuitive negotiator is the exact opposite to that of the analytical negotiator, as they often forgo the analytical phase:

— They proceed by perceiving the elements of the discussion by "gut feeling".
— They follow an emotional and an in-parallel mode of thought (several elements at the same time).
— They collect the information without analysing or organising it into a hierarchy before the decision suddenly crystallises.
— Their decision is reputed to be "implicit favourite" without it being necessarily nor objectively the best.

Intuitive profile is very frequently found in Oriental cultures, whereas in our western world it is found more commonly in the domain of sales reps.

It is difficult to expand upon the balance to be reached between these two types of behaviour as they are linked to the personality of the negotiator. However, an analytical negotiator should endeavour not to underestimate the information he can extract from his perception of the other, and to temper his analytical character when faced with an intuitive negotiator.

2.4 ASSERTIVE PROFILE VERSUS MANIPULATIVE PROFILE

The fourth type of behaviour is centred on the transparency (or lack of it) of the exchanges between the parties. At one extreme is assertive profile and at the other is the manipulative profile.

Assertive negotiators openly seek their ultimate goal:

— They clearly assert and adopt their positions.
— They speak clearly, concisely and unswervingly.
— They maintain a composed attitude, even when confronted with disagreement, criticism or conflict.
— They always treat people as their equals, irrespective of rank (higher or lower).
— They maintain an open and transparent position whilst remaining firm and determined.

Assertive behaviour is generally considered to be the most effective behaviour in negotiations. It is in any event the most transparent and most determined behaviour.

On the other hand, the manipulative negotiators continually act covertly but their objective is identical to that of the aggressive negotiator. They also seek a win-lose result, and never reveal their true intentions:

— They always conceal their objectives and motives.
— They continually try to persuade others to believe something that is not true.
— They do not clearly express their goals and if they do not reach them, they make the other person feel guilty.
— They appear to be listening, but in reality do not. They appear to agree when in fact, they don't. They approve or disapprove in silence without expressing an opinion.

Manipulative behaviour is often a form of fear of being exposed and confronted by the other person. It is as ineffective in the long term as aggressive behaviour, as people are generally only deceived once.

It goes without saying that assertive behaviour is the optimum behaviour that enables the best results, however, manipulation is very widespread and may turn out to be very effective when used skilfully and subtly.

Chapter 3

Negotiation style

Unless the approach is rational and planned, all individuals will react instinctively when placed in a negotiating situation, dependent not only upon their personality and approach to the negotiation, but also in relation to the circumstances in which they find themselves.

Yet, instinct naturally pushes the human being towards confrontation which can be counterproductive in negotiations, unless it is intentional and prepared. It is thus essential to understand the different styles in natural negotiation in order to interpret the reactions of the other party, or even to feign a natural approach to steer the negotiation to your advantage.

3.1 NEGOTIATION BASED ON COERCION

Negotiation style based on coercion relies on the willpower that one person imposes on the other. If the other person does not accept, they are exposed to an unavoidable outcome.

> **Mark:** ***Would a meeting at four suit you? I've got a problem that I need your help with.***
>
> **Patrick:** ***Four o'clock? No, that's not convenient! Lets say six. You'll just have to wait until then. Otherwise, you'll have to sort out your problem yourself.***
>
> **Mark:** ***Err, well, OK*** **[resentful].**

In the above case Mark needs Patrick to help him solve his problem. This gives Patrick a power that he uses to impose the time that he wants, without worrying whether it suits Mark. Mark has no alternative but to accept, otherwise Patrick will not help, although Mark clearly expressed an immediate need.

The systematic use of coercion is a short-term view as it provokes resentment in the person who is subjected to it and quickly elicits a desire for revenge.

However, it may be useful in certain cases when blocked, for example, in an intransigent situation.

3.2 NEGOTIATION BASED ON INTRANSIGENCE

Negotiation style based on intransigence lies on the refusal of a person to make any concessions. Either the other party accepts a win-lose result or breaks off the negotiations and ends up with a lose-lose outcome.

Philip: ***Would a briefing at five thirty suit you?***

Ann: ***Oh, no, I have to leave early. Let's meet halfway and say four thirty?***

Philip: ***No, it's not possible, five thirty or not at all!***

Ann: ***Oh, OK, five thirty it is then*** **[result lose-win to the detriment of Ann].**

Or

Ann: ***Too bad then, I can't come*** **[result lose-lose].**

In the above case Philip remains intransigent, adopting the "take it or leave it" attitude. Either Ann concedes and loses, or both parties lose.

When a negotiator systematically uses intransigence, sometimes it works and sometimes it doesn't. In the long term, the law of averages means that this negotiator only gets what they want half of the time, which is not very successful. Intransigence is only constructive if a negotiator does not necessarily need to reach an agreement. This is the case, for example, when a buyer has already found a supplier with whom they are prepared to sign; they can then negotiate intransigently with another supplier and if the negotiations are broken off, nothing is lost, and they then sign with the first supplier.

3.3 NEGOTIATION BASED ON MANIPULATION

Negotiation style based on manipulation relies on trickery. A person uses tricks to influence the other by making them believe untruths. The other person is cheated and accepts a win-lose result without realising it and to their detriment.

Mary: ***Would lunch at half one suit you? I would like to discuss my plan.***

Jack: ***Half one? I would find it difficult to hold on until then. Let's say half twelve?***

Mary: ***No, that won't be possible. I'm with my boss until half one*** **[lie].** ***But I would so much like to have lunch with you!***

Jack: ***Ah I see*** **[feeling guilty]*!*** ***OK, yes then.***

In the above case, Mary lies openly to make Jack feel guilty in order to have lunch with him at a time that suits her, rather than finding common ground. Feeling guilty, Jack concedes but how will he feel, for example, if he finds out that Mary's boss is on holiday that day?

No matter how reprehensible it might be, manipulation is a commonly used strategy in negotiations. It is particularly destructive for the relationship between the parties when discovered and if it is excessive. There is a real lack of consent, insofar as the other party would not have accepted the deal without such manipulation.

3.4 EXPRESS NEGOTIATION

Express negotiation style relies on the ability of a negotiator to proceed in such a manner that the other person is unable to put forward their points of view and are driven to accept the proposal. It is a form of negotiation avoidance.

Michael: ***I'll present my plan to you at six o'clock, OK?***

Alex: ***Ah, no chance. I have to get something from the shops...***

Michael: ***Come on! Forget the shops. It's very important. I've got a fantastic plan. OK?***

Alex: ***Well, err, no. You know, I have to...***

Michael: ***Come on, come on, you can go to the shops tomorrow. I'll come back to your office at six. You'll see, it's great*** **[leaving the room].**

Alex: ***Err, yes? Right, in fact... err... hmmm. [frustrated at having been pushed].***

In the above case Michael pressures Alex so fast that he apparently gets what he wants. Having said that, Alex has not really accepted the appointment. There is a high risk that Michael will find the door closed when he comes back at six, with Alex having gone.

As a general rule, expeditious negotiation only delays the resolution of the problem and negotiators often have to revert back to the subject. It is not a real negotiation, nevertheless this technique is regularly used to dismiss the less important points, when time is short, even if it means revisiting these points later.

3.5 NEGOTIATION BASED ON COMPROMISE

Negotiation style based on compromise relies on the principle of mutual concessions. One person takes a step, the other takes another step until they meet halfway. Halfway, yes... but the question is to know from where the negotiation stemmed. Indeed, one person might have started from an idealistic higher position while the other person might have started from a realistic lower position.

Peter: ***I'm glad that you want a copy of my latest book. The price is £50.***

John: ***£50? You don't say. It must be a future best seller at that price. Could you not make it £40 for a friend of 25 years?***

Peter: ***You've got a nerve, hey. Well, perhaps, for you, I could make it £45. OK?***

John: **Alright *[laughing].***

In the above case, Peter and John both make a concession of £5 and are apparently happy that the other has met him halfway. But who says that the price of £50 is not overpriced or that at £45 Peter is not making any real profit. Who says also that John does not want to buy Peter's book irrespective of the price.

Negotiation based on compromise is very common but very dangerous. First of all, it is the shrewdest who wins by setting goals at the start in order to obtain the desired margin without any loss. Often both parties are dissatisfied with the concessions made. Having said that, compromise is useful when the negotiators have completed the most difficult part of their negotiations, when they have relatively similar viewpoints and when one last push is all that is required... however, at this point, the last small effort becomes a fifty-fifty step.

3.6 NEGOTIATION BASED ON COLLABORATION

Negotiation style based on collaboration relies on the principle that the objectives of the various parties are not aggressive, or at least to a limited degree. Collaboration consists of openly negotiating the respective objectives and working towards a mutual solution that meets the majority, if not all the objectives. This generally ends up with a win-win result which is satisfactory to all parties and stands the test of time.

Nicole: ***Would lunch suit you at twelve today to finalise our contract? I'd like you to sign it tomorrow.***

Sylvia: ***Twelve? That'd be difficult as I've got a meeting at the end of the morning. I'd suggest one o'clock, even if it means continuing tomorrow. What do you think?***

Nicole: ***OK. But if we don't finalise it this lunchtime, we'll meet again tomorrow at twelve. OK?***

Sylvia: ***OK, by me. I'll book it in my diary for lunch tomorrow anyway, in case...***

In the above case, Nicole and Sylvia collaborate to find a solution that meets the desire of Nicole to get the contract signed the next day and the desire of Sylvia not to meet before one o'clock.

Negotiation based on collaboration often takes more time and energy, but is clearly the most effective.

Chapter 4

The reasoned approach

As you will have noticed, there is nothing instinctive or natural about effective negotiation. It is a question of strategies and techniques that each individual applies more or less correctly and on a regular basis according to their personality and inclinations.

If effective negotiation is not a question of an instinctive approach, then it must be a question of a reasoned approach.

4.1 THE BASIC FRAMEWORK

Negotiation is no more or no less than a process by which two or more parties make manoeuvres and concessions with respect to their starting positions, a priori divergent, in order to align their points of view and reach an agreement.

The art of negotiation consists entirely of discovering and concentrating on convergent interests... and, of course, using the negotiating surrounding space to the best or their interests.

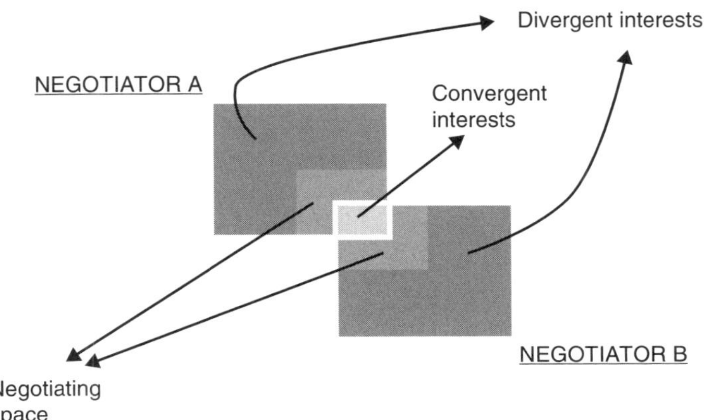

4.2 THE 4C METHOD

The 4C method is a reasoned approach aimed at systematising the use of negotiating principles:

— Negotiation profiles and negotiation styles.
— Steps in the negotiation process.
— Possible strategies.
— Negotiation techniques.

However, these negotiating principles can only become a worthwhile set of tools if they are accompanied by a method explaining how to use them. The 4C method (Compose – Clarify – Confront – Commit) helps you to achieve this ambitious objective.

Part 2

NEGOTIATION PROCESS

Chapter 1

The steps of the process

An accomplished negotiator concentrates as much on the negotiation procedure as on its content. Indeed, negotiating strategies and techniques only have the desired outcome if they are used at the appropriate time.

1.1 THE SEQUENTIAL PROCEDURE

In a negotiation, there is a sequence of nine steps as follows:

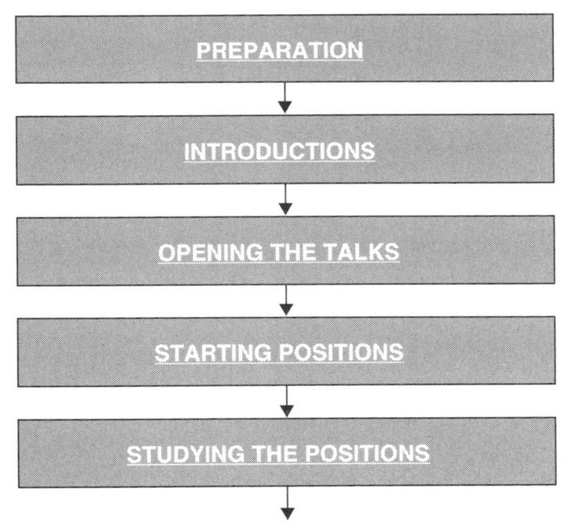

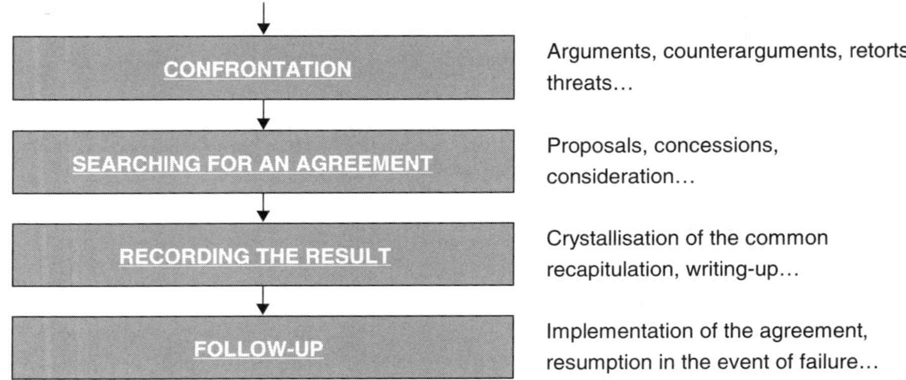

1.2 PREPARATION

Preparing the negotiation is an essential step. The more care in the preparation, the easier the negotiation will be with the supplier. This preparation covers primarily two distinct areas:

1. Compiling a case file containing the objective and quantitative elements: the supplier's offer, the breakdown of the sales price, competing offers, supplier's profile as well as the profile of those involved in the negotiation, annual accounts to assess financial health, etc.
2. Planning the negotiation: objectives, negotiable points, anticipating room for manoeuvre, arguments, possible concessions, choice of participants, agenda, envisaged strategy, anticipated techniques, scenario of the meeting, etc.

1.3 INTRODUCTIONS

Introductions are often hurried, making it necessary to rapidly identify the position and level of power of each person. Knowing the position within the organisation is an important aspect as it can reveal upfront their insight and their decision power and whether attention should be paid to their every word.

Introductions also help to identify the role each person will play in the negotiation process, the key role being, of course, the chairperson.

Finally, introductions provide an opportunity to seat the participants perhaps based on a predefined seating plan, be it official or unofficial, or on a specific or non-specific strategy.

1.4 OPENING THE TALKS

At the opening of the discussions, the terms of reference of the negotiation should be defined in order to avoid losing sight of the focal point and to ensure that everybody is on the same wavelength:

- — Meeting objectives.
- — Agenda.
- — Timing.
- — Rules of play.

1.5 STARTING POSITIONS

This step consists of the parties defining their starting position. The question is who should be the first to define their position? As a general rule, it is the one who is on the lookout for something, for example, the customer who is looking for a new supplier, the supplier who wants to increase his prices, the customer who wants to adjust the prices downwards, etc.

While one party sets out their viewpoints, the other listens, takes notes and formulates questions for clarification.

In principle, this step is concluded by a recapitulation of the positions that have already been communicated. This should be the role of the chairman, whether it be someone, as such elected at the onset, or someone who has slipped quite naturally into the chairing role.

1.6 STUDYING THE POSITIONS

As its name suggests, studying the positions consists of each party analysing the position of the other in terms of:

- — Points of convergence vis-à-vis their own position.
- — Points of divergence requiring discussion.
- — Items of an unspoken nature, often weighing heavily on the negotiation.
- — Contradictions that reveal true motives.
- — Tricks that highlight one or another strategy.

If the negotiator is alone, this analysis can be carried out during the course of the meeting or alternatively, at a private break out session. The objective is to prepare for the oncoming offensive.

1.7 CONFRONTATION

Prior to the confrontation of starting positions, there is an artificial equilibrium between the parties and their positions. The purpose of the confrontation is to break this artificial equilibrium in order to find a new and more representative balance between the opposing parties and this, based on their unwavering points of view and the relevance of their arguments:

— Arguments and counter-arguments.
— Mutual retorts.
— Threats and promises.
— Non-verbal and body language.

Only at the end of the confrontation, when all the cards are on the table, can one really measure the true importance of the divergent views and the influence of each party.

1.8 SEARCHING FOR AN AGREEMENT

The quest to reach an agreement consists of bringing closer together divergent points of view by:

— Making proposals for alternatives and counter proposals.
— Accepting concessions.
— Getting something in return.
— Regularly recapitulating the points of agreement as levers.
— Frequent reminders of the concessions made.

1.9 RECORDING THE RESULT

Recording the result is a formal declaration based on either an agreement or a continuing disagreement, giving the parties time to consider the situation before accepting the outcome.

In principle, the outcome is officialised by drawing up an assessment of the observations and decisions established during the course of the meeting.

1.10 FOLLOW-UP

The follow-up to the negotiation consists of implementing the agreement or subsequently resuming the negotiation in the event of failure. In principle, at the end of the previous step, the actions to be taken are identified and decided on.

Chapter 2

The procedural strategies

The purpose of procedural strategies is to influence the order of the discussions and to lead them in a favourable direction for one or the other party.

2.1 THE SALAMI

This strategy consists of cutting the negotiation up into sections and negotiating the different sections in sequence.

The points to be negotiated are thus grouped together into chapters or sections as in the following example:

Agenda

A. Delivery
- **1) Delivery period**
- **3) Delivery Duty Paid or Ex-Works**
- **4) Delivery notice or reception notice**

B. Prices
- **1) Minimum quantity**
- **2) Unit price per 10, 15 and more**
- **3) End of year discount**

C. Payment conditions
- **1) Payment terms**
- **2) Cash discount**

The points within each section can be negotiated at the same time, however, the rules of the game are, for example, that section B will only be dealt with when agreement has been reached on section A. This strategy facilitates regular recourse to the ultimatum: *"no point in moving on to another section before having reached agreement on this one"*.

It is important that the sections are organised in such a manner that items impacting those that follow are negotiated first. For example, it is pointless discussing the price when there has been no decision on whether delivery is carriage paid or ex-works.

2.2 FOLLOW THE FLOW

This strategy consists of negotiating the various points in the order set out in the draft document, which is being used as the basis for the negotiation, and on condition it follows the logic defined by the authors of the document.

Very often the draft document is a draft contract, for example:

Draft Contract

1. **Parties to the contract**
2. **Subject of the contract**
3. **Description of the products**
4. **Prices of the products**
5. **Order conditions**
6. **Delivery conditions**
7. **Quarterly and annual discounts**
8. **Payment conditions and penalties**
9. **Warranty clause**

This strategy accelerates the entire process as the negotiation relates directly to a text that is as close as possible to any future agreement, in this case the contract.

On the other hand, this strategy can lead to similar items being in different chapters rendering the negotiation more difficult for the participants. In the above example, this is the case for the prices and discounts that are given in chapters 4 and 7 respectively.

2.3 GIVE AND TAKE

The give and take strategy consists of grouping the items to be negotiated and the reciprocal concessions into balanced "packages":

Agenda

- **A. Order conditions**
  - **1) Order frequency**
  - **2) Minimum order quantity**
- **B. Delivery conditions**
  - **1) Delivery lead time**
  - **2) Delivery arrangements**
- **C. Financial conditions**
  - **1) Unit price**
  - **2) End of year discount**
  - **3) Payment terms**

This strategy relies on the ability of the negotiator to combine the items into attractive packages, such that a final agreement will be considered profitable for both parties.

In the above example and in order to reduce their stock, the customer wants the most frequent orders, with the smallest order quantities possible, whereas the supplier would rather ensure a minimum quantity for each order.

2.4 ENDURANCE

The endurance strategy consists of playing for time and making the negotiation last by applying the Pareto principle whereby 80% of concessions are made in the last 20% of the time.

The tools used are of course, marathon exchanges, interruptions and adjournments.

As time progresses, the more inexperienced negotiators become impatient and are more inclined to make concessions in order to conclude.

Chapter 3

Decision strategies

The purpose of decision strategies is to influence the decision-making process of the other person, to obtain a faster and more favourable decision, rather than follow the path of their own normal decision-making process.

3.1 THE "PULL" AND THE "PUSH"

The purpose of the strategy of alternating between "pull" and "push" is to prompt the other party into making earlier than planned concessions.

In principle, the "pull" is used to convey to the other person that you are on their side, with a view to drawing them as closely as possible to your own position:

— Firstly by establishing confidence and by searching for common ground.

— Then by making an attractive proposal, defending it enthusiastically and perhaps even adopting a friendly behaviour.

The "push" is used to pressurise and undermine the other party and to push them to change their position:

— Firstly by attempting to persuade them by presenting a proposal and a strong argument.

— Then by applying assurance and firmness with assertive behaviour or, if necessary, even a slightly aggressive approach.

To represent this pull-push strategy, people often use the image of a person entrenched in their position and then pulled and pushed, back and forth, in the same way that a tree trunk is uprooted.

3.2 THE 4 STEPS

The strategy of the 4 steps consists of encouraging the other person to finally adopt a position that they will regard as favourable while in reality, it will only be a slight improvement on what there were initially trying to avoid.

The 4 positions or steps are:

1. Ideal position for yourself but intolerable for the other person.
2. Excellent position for yourself and acceptable to the other person.
3. Minimum or fallback position for yourself.
4. Intolerable position for yourself but ideal for the other person.

The negotiator opens with step 4, rejects it immediately such that the other party no longer considers it as an ideal position.

The negotiator then details step 3, identifies the disadvantages and the reasons for not accepting. The objective is to push the other party to consider step 3 as their ideal position on the basis of which they make concessions.

The negotiator then starts the real negotiation with step 1, aiming for step 2.

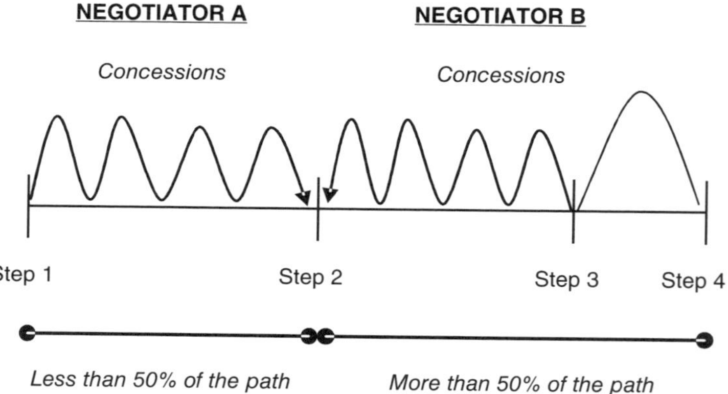

In conclusion, if the negotiation turns into a simple compromise and the parties "meet each other halfway" on their respective positions, i.e. steps 1 and 3, negotiator A, who applied this strategy, will have made fewer concessions than negotiator B.

3.3 THE APPLICATION OF FORCE

As the name suggests, the application of force strategy consists of forcing the other person's hand by being the strongest, asserting yourself and your position.

This strategy is founded on the intentional convergence of expeditious negotiation and aggressive and dominating behaviours. The aim is to stop the other person putting forward their point of view by proceeding quickly, aggressively and/or by dominating the situation.

The negotiator who applies it uses 4 tactics in particular:

- Methodical demonstration (analysis, argument, deduction, conclusion, generalisation).
- Insistence (repetition of information) and evidence (use of proverbs, examples, judgements).
- Threats (a clear or veiled promise of retaliation in the event of rejection).
- Body effect (extensive movements, direct gaze) and verbal effect (high tone, controlled rapid delivery).

The following reaction would be a typical example. *"It's as easy as ABC"*, he said. *"I've made enough concessions for an hour, and I'm not making any more. If you refuse this last offer, I will be compelled to take you off our supplier list"*, he exclaimed getting up from his chair and banging his fist on the table.

Chapter 4

Manipulative strategies

The purpose of manipulative strategies is to influence the decision-making process of the other person by employing camouflage and stratagems to take advantage of them and to lead them, without their knowledge, to a solution that they would not have otherwise chosen.

4.1 THE DECOY

The strategy of the decoy consists of making the other person believe that one point of the negotiation is crucial, with an unacceptable demand, when in fact it is secondary.

The person who employs this strategy will subsequently abandon all ambitions in this respect... but will ensure, nevertheless, a good payback, this being the purpose of the game. The other person will be relieved to resolve the dilemma as, in spite of it all, the price paid will be lower than the initial demand.

A typical example is the following. Harnet & Sons are the largest distributor of office furniture in the south of the country, however, their competitor in the north, Top Office, is not to be taken for granted. The producer Linea PLC had just presented a new office range to Harnet & Sons to be distributed throughout the country. Harnet & Sons were interested but immediately demanded exclusivity to distribute this new range throughout the territory, arguing the need for a large volume of business in order to recoup the advertising costs. This put Linea PLC in a serious predicament as they needed Harnet & Sons for business in the south of the country, but they also needed Top Office for the north. For almost an hour Harnet & Sons maintained their position before concluding that if exclusivity was not possible, the £50,000 for the advertising campaign would have to be paid by Linea PLC. Too happy to resolve the problem of exclusivity, Linea PLC accepted... without realising that this is what Harnet & Sons were aiming for in the initial stage.

4.2 THE UNDERLING

The underling strategy is a manipulation that consists of making the other person believe that the negotiator is not the decision-maker. This strategy is also called the fall guy technique.

As a matter of routine, negotiators never present themselves as decision-makers otherwise their verbal agreement would leave them no issue. It is more cunning, on their part, to indicate that they have to refer to a higher authority for final approval. They note the points of the negotiation, the arguments and the alternatives and after considering all the facts and taking the time to evaluate the ins and outs of situation, they return with an appropriate negotiating strategy.

They then behave as if they are negotiating on behalf of a third party and if something unexpected comes up, use the excuse of firstly having to consult the decision-maker. This tactic gives them time to reconsider the situation and adapt their strategy accordingly. It can even open the door to the possibility of putting everything into question again... because supposedly the pseudo decision-maker does not agree.

When confronted with such a negotiator, it is in the interest of the other party to request a meeting and to negotiate directly with the decision-maker. Faced with such a request, the negotiator who uses this strategy will hold out for as long as they can, and will then be forced to come out of their sanctuary and return to a more open attitude.

4.3 GOOD COP, BAD COP

The "good cop, bad cop" strategy consists of clearly creating complicity with the other person, taking their side to better influence them.

The technique is as old as the hills. The buyer takes on the role of "good cop" and negotiates normally understanding in full the problems of the seller. However, there is the buyer's boss, the "bad cop" (if he really exists), who is not present and wants nothing to do with the negotiation. The consequence is twofold. On the one hand, complicity is established between the buyer and seller but on the other hand, a series of back and forth exchanges can lead to additional concessions on the part of the seller. The latter come from the role played by the "good cop", however, there is never a "good cop" without a "bad cop".

The role of the "bad cop" is to always ask for more but not to the extent of excessive demands where the other party could consider breaking off negotiations. On the other side, the "good cop" is always there ready to calm the situation, sympathise and come up with proposals... not as exaggerated as those of the "bad cop", nevertheless more than the other party was prepared to accept in the initial stage.

The success of this strategy is thus measured by the skill of the "good cop", and not by that of the "bad cop", who is there to upset the other party, leading them to revise their positions thereby enabling the "good cop" to profit. In this type of situation, be more wary of the "good cop" than of the "bad cop".

4.4 THE FALSE PRETEXT

The false pretext strategy is a manipulation that puts pressure on the conditions that you want to obtain from the supplier (e.g. the price) or on the negotiation procedure (e.g. timing). Two false pretexts are great classics.

The extremely short deadline, preferably impossible, imposed upon the seller to obtain the goods or services in question, is the favourite false pretext of buyers... to reduce the price to compensate for the inconvenience of a longer deadline. The only delicate point is arguing the case for the extremely short deadline, as the seller will only fall for it if the situation is plausible.

The false appointment is another one of the great classics of buyers to accelerate the progress of the negotiation and to make the seller decide in haste, example *"I'll be seeing my boss at the end of the day to make a decision"*.

4.5 THE ALLIANCE

The search for an alliance is another great classic in manipulative strategies. It is formidably effective when more than two parties are negotiating (or are around the table).

The principle is to initiate prior contact with another potential "ally" to join forces (officially or unofficially) and to take turns in the negotiations... agreeing beforehand on the concessions-compensation acceptable to both parties.

As an example, take a building site wanting to re-equip one of the floors with office furniture involving contacting several suppliers, A is responsible for the desks, and B for the seats.

The starting situation is as follows:

- For A the period required to assemble the furniture is a minimum of one week. Less than one week would require more fitters than A has available resulting in a need to take on extra external fitters. A delivery period of 3 to 4 weeks, effective the signing date of the order, could perhaps be revised downwards and the access to the site could be by an internal lift or an external goods lift available to A, or alternatively, by the stairs.
- For B, the delivery period of one month is very important, without which B will have to use temporary agency staff, who are less productive, to accelerate production. The assembly duration could however, be reduced to one day as there is no real assembly involved in the chairs. The method for accessing the site is of little importance to B.

Prior to the negotiation with the customer and the cabinet supplier, A and B had a meeting together and agreed that:

- The assembly period will be a minimum of one week (requirement of A that B will support).
- The delivery period will be one month (requirement of B, to which B has added a small safety margin, and that A will support in return).

- The method for accessing the site can be by the lift, or by stairs, or even by the external goods lift, in return for a supplement for the machine and its operator.

In conclusion, there is no leeway left for the last supplier other than to negotiate the last point. As you will see, an alliance is often a search for the lowest common denominator... to the detriment of the other party.

Part 3

NEGOTIATING TECHNIQUES

Chapter 1

The tools

Negotiating techniques are manoeuvres aimed at challenging the starting position of the other party with a view to inciting them to revise their position. These negotiating techniques include tools, tricks and ploys.

The tools are extensive negotiating techniques, used openly and with an effectiveness which is widely acknowledged.

1.1 COMPETITIVE LEVERAGE

You can only have good commercial negotiations if each seller is aware that they are faced with serious competitors who also want to win the contract, thus competing with each other to the benefit of the buyer.

As a minimum, each seller should be informed that they are competing with others and, preferably, be given their names to increase the credibility of the competition. Slipping in the name of a competitor, renowned for slashing prices, can be used as a ploy.

An appropriate move is to give regular feedback to the seller regarding their position vis-à-vis the competition, in the following manner:

- — Semi-open by giving general information (e.g. around 5% more expensive than the seller offering the best deal).
- — Open, by giving precise information (e.g. £1.73 more expensive than SPEED for a ream of 500 sheets).
- — Transparent by presenting the results of the evaluation:

SUPPLY OF PHOTOCOPY PAPER							
CRITERIA		**SPEED**		**SUPPLIER 2**		**SUPPLIER 3**	
ELIMINATION:							
a) A4 format - 80 g - quality D		Yes	–	Yes	–	Yes	–
b) Inkjet & photocopier compatible		Yes	–	Yes	–	Yes	–
c) Minimum order quantity of box maximum		Yes	–	No	(5 boxes minimum)	Yes	–
EVALUATION:	WEIGHT:						
1. Delivery lead time	3	< 24 h	10 pts			24-48 h	8 pts
2. Delivery type	5	Offices	8 pts			Cabinets	10 pts
3. Price per ream of 500	4	£4,49	8 pts			£5,22	4 pts
4. Payment terms	4	Upon invoice	4 pts			60 days	8 pts
			118 pts				122 pts

DELIVERY LEAD TIME		DELIVERY TYPE		PRICE PER REAM OF 500		PAYMENT TERMS	
< 24h	10 pts	Collection	0 pts	< £4,00	10 pts	Upon order	0 pts
24-48h	8 pts	Delivery to the bay	2 pts	£4,00 – £4,50	8 pts	Upon delivery	2 pts
3 days	6 pts	Delivery to reception	4 pts	£4,50 – £5,00	6 pts	Upon invoice	4 pts
4 days	4 pts	Delivery to the floors	6 pts	£5,00 – £5,50	4 pts	30 days	6 pts
5 days	2 pts	Delivery to the offices	8 pts	£5,50 – £6,00	2 pts	60 days	8 pts
> 5 days	0 pts	Resupply of cabinets	10 pts	> £6,00	0 pts	> 60 days	10 pts

All of the latter can be applied and are acceptable on condition they remain legal, honest and over and above board.

For example, the lowest bid system, by internet or other, gives amazing results and can show that sellers have greater manoeuvring room which is generally more than originally perceived. It is not the highest bid but the lowest bid that wins. If there are not too many sellers, a good practical rule is to keep the best starting offer in hand and leave the remaining offers to bid one against the other. This technique facilitates dealing with extreme situations whereby sellers refuse to play the bidding game or where a certain collusion has developed between the remaining sellers. Under these circumstances, the buyer can always revert back to the original offer put on hold.

1.2 SEATING PLAN

The seating plan (intentional or unintentional) reveals the spirit of the forthcoming negotiation. In this respect it becomes a tool of crucial importance... and at no cost.

The commonest seating plans are:

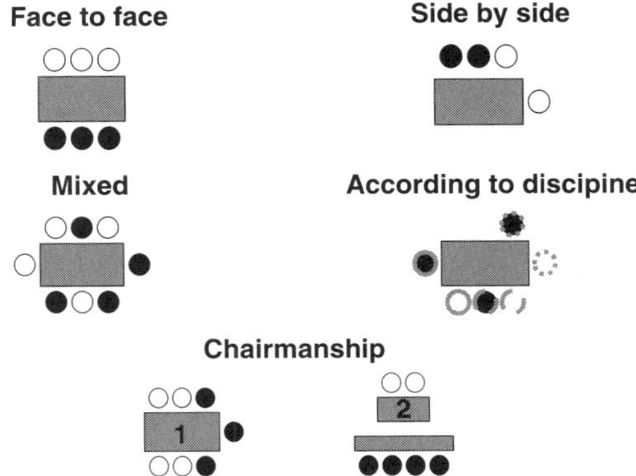

Each seating plan corresponds to a particular tactic:

- Face to face is clearly conducive to conflict, even aggression.
- Side by side on the other hand is convivial.
- Mixed and grouping by discipline fosters collaboration.
- Chairmanship – version 1 shows a desire to dominate on the part of the black team, and chairmanship – version 2 also adds a conflicting even aggressive dimension.

It is thus essential to strengthen the chosen strategy with the appropriate seating plan.

1.3 RELEVANT QUESTIONING

Questioning denotes the way in which the questions are posed and becomes a relevant tool when used to obtain the desired information, and to also adapt the method of communication to the appropriate phase in the negotiation:

TYPE OF QUESTION	OBJECTIVE	EXAMPLE
1. OPEN QUESTIONS	Open the dialogue Obtain information	Who does..., why do you..., how does hat, when do we...
2. CLOSED QUESTIONS	Verify the facts Test your understanding	Is it true that... Have I understood correctly...
3. ANALYTICAL QUESTIONS	Clarify the position Challenge preconceived ideas Obtain proof	Why do you hink hat... What makes you believe that... Do you have proof of...
4. QUESTIONS REQUIRING CONSIDERATION	Find solu ions Explore new paths	If we agree, how do we... and if we do....
5. ALTERNATIVE QUESTIONS	Propose a choice Find agreement	Who could do it best... Would you prefer... or...

In general, questions can be categorised under the following negotiation phases:

- Open questions: usually during the introductions, opening the dialogue and setting out the starting positions.
- Closed questions: more appropriate at the time of recapitulation of the starting positions and the confrontation.
- Analytical questions: often used during the confrontation phase.
- Questions requiring consideration and alternative questions: should be reserved to wrap up loose ends in the agreement stage.

1.4 EMPATHY

Empathy is a concept defined by the German psychologist Lipps (1851-1914), which means "feeling within":

- Immersing yourself in the subjective world of the other person.
- Listening to and understanding their logic.
- Being sensitive to their reactions and managing them.
- Controlling your own emotions.
- Concentrating on the heart of the matter.

This concept was popularised in 1960 by the American psychologist Rogers, further to which empathy became a true communication tool at work. In negotiations too, empathy is largely considered as a tool:

- The friendly negotiator shows empathy with respect to the other person, as it is second nature to them.
- The assertive negotiator also shows empathy but more intentionally, knowing the positive effect that it can have on the negotiation process.
- The manipulative negotiator often shows empathy but only to influence things in their direction.

1.5 ATTACK-DEFENCE SPIRAL

In the event of criticism or attack, the natural reaction is to defend oneself by counter criticism and attack... generally emotions and ego get the upper hand. This type of behaviour is highly counterproductive during negotiations.

Knowing how to avoid this attack-defence spiral is a powerful tool for the negotiator who recognises the difference between the problems and the people, or when confronted with an aggressive negotiator... apply the following strategic approach:

- Listen, understand and evaluate before answering.
- If the criticism is correct, acknowledge it.
- If the criticism is incorrect, express disagreement and justify briefly.
- Resist the desire to immediately counterattack, even with the appropriate arguments on hand, but come back to the matter at a more opportune moment.

If no action is taken to avoid such a conflict, the attack-defence spiral will have unbalanced influences on the relationship between the two parties:

REACTION OF THE PERSON ATTACKED	REACTION OF THE AGGRESSOR	NATURE OF THE RELATIONSHIP
REFUSES THE SPIRAL	Mistrust	Rebalance of the relationship
HOSTILE ATTITUDE	Hostile attitude	Long term aggressive relationship
MORE HOSTILE ATTITUDE	1) Withdrawal 2) Escalation	1) Rebalance of the relationship 2) Antagonistic & violent relationship
NO REACTION	Continues the aggression to test the vulnerability of the other	Changing and uncertain relationship
SUBMISSION	Increases the aggression	Dominant-submissive relationship

1.6 ANALYSIS OF THE COST PRICE

COST ITEMS	VOLUME		AMOUNT	
Building costs	**Quantity**	**Unit**	**£/m²**	**£ p.a.**
Warehouse	8,500	sqm(s)	£5.10	£520,200.00
Offices	220	sqm(s)	£6.00	£15,840.00
Charges				£71,818.00
s/total				**£607,858.00**
Labour costs	**Quantity**	**Unit**	**£/month**	**£ p.a.**
Site Manager	1.0	FTE(s)	£6,588.00	£79,056.00
Operators	11.0	FTE(s)	£2,634.00	£347,688.00
Administration	2.0	FTE(s)	£2,821.00	£67,704.00
s/total				**£494,448.00**
Equipment costs	**Quantity**	**Unit**	**£/month**	**£ p.a.**
Forklift truck	3	machine(s)	£750.00	£27,000.00
Electric pallet truck	5	machine(s)	£563.00	£33,780.00
Film wrapping machine	1	machine(s)	£1,230.00	£14,760.00
s/total				**£75,540.00**
TOTAL				**£1,177,846.00**
Fixed amounts	**Quantity**	**Unit**	**£/month**	**£ p.a.**
Building, equipment, permanent staff	12	month(s)	£81,792.04	£981,504.48
s/total				**£981,504.48**
Variable amounts	**Quantity**	**Unit**	**£/unit**	**£ p.a.**
Reception & stockage of pallets	42,000	pallet(s)	£3.50	£147,000.00
Pick, pack & load (per piece)	1,130,000	piece(s)	£0.34	£384,200.00
Pick, pack & load (per pallet)	10,675	pallet(s)	£2.61	£27,861.75
s/total				**£559,061.75**
TOTAL				**£1,540,566.23**

An important part of any commercial negotiation is linked to the price, not just the total, but to a comprehensive breakdown. The more detailed the breakdown on the sales price, the closer it will come to the cost price of the seller and the more points of discussion and arguments will emerge for the buyer.

When negotiating an important contract, it is customary to send the potential sellers a standard form, requesting they complete every section (e.g. quantity, unit, amount per unit and annual amount). The following example has been taken from an existing document and is relative to a logistics contract for the delivery, storage, preparation and loading of goods.

To encourage the seller to communicate this information in full, the buyer can use the pretext that it would help in improving their offer by not only reviewing together their working hypotheses (e.g. units), but also other aspects of business.

The truth of the matter being that the underlying value of such a document is to enable the buyer to challenge the seller on each item and to be in a position to back up their arguments. Another benefit is that it highlights the seller's profit margins (invoicing – costs).

1.7 ROOM FOR MANOEUVRE

It is essential to have a clear picture of the seller as a player on the market: their product positioning, their annual accounts, their brochures, etc. In this respect, the annual accounts are a source of information that is traditionally underused. By revealing their overall gross margin, they are put in the position whereby they must demonstrate that their margin is less for the product in question.

It is also essential to identify your own objectives in the negotiation, i.e. what you want to obtain from the seller and to identify the seller's objectives as quickly as possible. In any event, the points most likely to be negotiated must be prepared ahead of time so as to not be caught off guard during the negotiation.

Building in adequate room for manoeuvre is thus an essential tool which enables moderating your requirements to obtain something in return:

- Identify the negotiable points or objectives of the negotiation during the preparation phase.
- Identify the ideal requirements with which you will open the negotiation, as well as the realistic requirements for which you are aiming, and your fall-back position should agreement not be reached and negotiations broken off.
- List and prepare the arguments.

NEGOCIABLE POINT	IDEAL REQUIREMENT	REALISTIC REQUIREMENT	FALLBACK REQUIREMENT	ARGUMENTS
Delivery lead time	24-48 h	3 working days	> 5 working days	– The competition is 24-48h – SPEED is < 24h - Our need for flexibility will otherwise make us keep a second supplier
Price per ream of 500	< £4.50	< £5.00	> £5.50	– Our purchasing volume is 1,000 reams per month – The existence of a minimum order quantity
Payment term	90 days end of month	60 days end of month	< 60 days end of month	– Our strong financial situation – The absence of suitable discount for cah payment

1.8 ARGUMENTATION

It is extremely rare that a spontaneous argument, in the heat of the moment, can be effective. In order to be effective, an argument must satisfy as many as possible of the following criteria, all of which require preparation:

- Relevant, as an argument weighs more in the balance if it touches a sensitive point for the other party.
- Specific, as in this case it shows the expertise of the negotiator who uses it.
- Objective, as an argument is difficult to contest if it is based on demonstrable data.
- Original, as such an argument is unforeseeable and thus difficult to refute.
- Concise, as a long argument leads the other party to lose track and generally fizzles out. Moreover, it gives the other party time to prepare a counter-argument.

This process is all the more effective if the negotiator has prepared a number of arguments, without which unnecessary repetition will take place during the confrontation stage, giving an impression of weaknesses in the arguments. The more arguments a negotiator has in hand, the easier it is for him to counteract the arguments of the other party.

1.9 CONCESSION-COMPENSATION

The easiest way to get something in return is to ask for compensation from a seller who is pressing the buyer to make a concession. It is then the seller who takes the first step and becomes the asker.

This approach has a dual purpose as it quickly discourages the seller from repeatedly coming back to the subject of further concessions. It must be emphasised that concessions enable the differing positions to come together but these concessions must be of a mutual and balanced nature.

The best preparation for this type of technique is obviously to prepare a matrix of concessions-compensations:

CONCESSION	COMPENSATION
– Payment 60 days instead of 90 days	Additional discount of 1%
– Payment 30 days instead of 90 days	Additional discount of 2%
– **Cash payment**	**Additional discount of 8%**
– Minimum order quantity	Reduce delivery lead time to 48 hours

As you can see, you can continue until further concessions-compensation become impossible. For example, rather than replying "no" to a seller who is asking for immediate payment, you can ask for an additional discount of 8%, to which he will inevitably say "no". Thus the buyer is not really refusing and places the responsibility of the "no" onto the seller.

1.10 PARTICIPANTS

The number of participants who speak at any given moment is a tool that can increase the outcome of the dialogue. In general, a single participant focuses the adverse party on the content of the dialogue and amplifies its importance. In the reverse situation, a multitude of participants dilutes the content and importance of the words and gives the effect of an onslaught.

When opening the negotiation (introductions, studying the starting positions), it is more effective to have a single participant opening the dialogue:

- Either the most senior person, to benefit from their authority, power or charisma.
- Or the rank just below, to bring about a build-up effect.

During the confrontation phase, all the participants make their point, one after the other, without leaving the other party time to catch their breath.

During the conciliation phase, the same single participant searches for common ground and proposes solutions.

1.11 CALLING OUT OF BOUNDS

The behaviour of a person during the negotiation process can go beyond the bounds of acceptability vis-à-vis the other party and not necessarily solely due to the fact that the negotiator is of an aggressive, dominating or manipulative nature.

It is commonly accepted that certain behaviour goes against common morals, laws and regulations, business ethics, respect for people, etc:

- Personal attack.
- Intimidation.

— Bad faith.
— Lying.
— Physical threats.
— Blackmail.
— Coercion.
— Corruption.
— Defamation.
— Unfounded criticism.
— Blatant exaggeration.

It is a moral duty not to accept the unacceptable, and also a rule of good practice in all negotiations. In fact, going beyond the limits, unbalances the negotiation process such that an agreement becomes impossible to reach.

The reaction to this type of behaviour must be immediate, firm, and above all, dispassionate. Reasoned escalation is a simple and effective tool in 3 steps:

1. Natural prevention, which consists of avoiding provocative attitudes as much as possible: controversy, application of force, manipulation, attack-defence spirals, etc, which often incite reactions which in turn go beyond the limits of the acceptable.
2. Refocusing, which consists of interrupting the course of the negotiation in the face of unacceptable behaviour in order to go over the rules of play again and to give a clear warning to those concerned.
3. Disqualification, which consists of breaking off negotiations if the unacceptable behaviour continues and asking for another negotiator.

1.12 BREAKING OFF NEGOTIATIONS

The freedom to contract or not, is a golden rule never to be forgotten, as long as a firm agreement between parties has not been reached.

If at the point of concluding and the buyer again experiences a feeling of dissatisfaction, the last resort is still open to break off the negotiation. It is the best way to put enormous pressure on the seller who has but a single choice: make an additional concession or take responsibility (in the face of their boss, for example) for the failure of the negotiation.

Breaking off negotiations can also be used as a tool provided you do not burn your bridges behind you. In this way, the seller has time to return to the game with a new element and the two parties can resume negotiations without losing face.

Chapter 2

Tricks and ploys

Contrary to tools, tricks & ploys are more emotional negotiating techniques whose usage and effectiveness come more from the personality and expertise of the negotiator using them.

2.1 PARETO PRINCIPLE

The Pareto principle is perfectly applicable to negotiations insofar that 80% of concessions are made in the last 20% of the negotiating time.

The ploy of opening the negotiation with either high demands, or alternatively one single demand, helps focus attention and averts reaching too early discussions on the real issues. In the same way as it is appropriate to take advantage of the approaching conclusion to raise problems hostile to this agreement.

The extreme case of this principle is what buyers call the "Colombo effect" which consists of raising a last stumbling block just prior to concluding ("Oh, by the way...") in order to get a bit more... however, on the express condition that you are prepared for a probable refusal by the seller. In this case, two options are open to the buyer, assuming their decision was defined at the very start:

— Be a good sport: *"OK, I understand, but nothing ventured, nothing gained, don't you think?"*

— Break off the negotiation with a view to actually getting what you want: *"Right, too bad, otherwise it would have been done and I would have signed the contract."*

2.2 NEVER DISPLAY ENTHUSIASM

It is a basic rule to never display enthusiasm when approaching a seller, although this trick is rarely used. Indeed, it is not the role of the buyer to facilitate the job of the seller whose role it is to convince and sell.

By displaying scepticism, lack of enthusiasm, indecision and preference for a competitor, the seller is compelled to surpass himself and "hold nothing back". In any case, it is a fundamental error to imply that the decision has already been made, or is on the brink of being made.

2.3 NEVER ACCEPT THE FIRST OFFER

Although it does not happen as often as we would like, in some cases the first offer made by a seller is bang on or even better than the initial target. There is a great temptation to just stretch out your hand and say *"OK, sold!"*.

In fact, accepting the first offer can turn out to be frustrating for both parties as it leaves no opportunity for the negotiation to develop:

— The buyer subsequently risks regretting not having negotiated to get something even better.

— The seller also risks regretting not having offered less.

In such cases, and if the occasion arises, it is quite common for either party to question the terms of the agreement (e.g. *"We're sorry, but a mistake inadvertently slipped into our specifications or our tender..."*). A good trick is to therefore automatically reject the first offer.

2.4 NON-VERBAL BEHAVIOUR

Another obvious trick, seldom employed, is to never acknowledge that an offer is attractive, cheaper than a competitor, etc.

When the price is revealed, non-verbal behaviour such as huffing and puffing, displaying a surprised or disbelieving expression, shaking of the head, rubbing of the forehead and other body language can be extremely effective. In fact they do not necessarily prompt a visible reaction from the seller who considers these reactions as subconscious signals from the buyer. On the other hand, phrases such as *"How much?"*, *"What?"*, *"Have I misunderstood?"* are effective, but will require a response from the seller.

Not reacting to the price is to indirectly indicate to the seller that this price has been accepted and there is nothing more to do than to discuss the other components of the offer.

2.5 ALWAYS ASK FOR THE IMPOSSIBLE

An unbelievably effective trick, but difficult psychologically if you are not used to it, is to first ask for the impossible.

Firstly because, although excessive, the demand can sometimes tally with what the seller is prepared to give up. Also because it gives greater room for manoeuvre during the rest of the negotiation and can demonstrate a spirit of conciliation on the part of the buyer. Finally, concessions by the buyer give the seller the impression that they have also succeeded in the negotiation.

2.6 MUST DO A LOT BETTER

Firstly and most importantly, this is a ploy that enables the buyer, once the seller has announced the price, to immediately return the ball to the other court and compels the seller to justify the price and, in many cases, to make a concession.

An anecdote beautifully illustrates this ploy, although there may be more myth than historic truth in the story. When Henry Kissinger was Nixon's Secretary of State, he asked one of his advisers to draw up an analysis and to make a recommendation for his next meeting with the President. After several days of hard labour, the adviser gave Secretary Kissinger a detailed report and a recommendation with an explanatory note asking for an appointment to discuss it face to face. The sole reply that he got back was his original report with the following sentence from the Secretary of State on the cover: *"You'll have to do a lot better than that. H.K."*. The adviser got back to work, revised his report and refined his recommendation. It was much to his surprise to see his report come back again with the same laconic note. This time the adviser redoubled his efforts and completed his report with an impressive series of material arguments that he considered irrefutable. He did not make the same mistake of putting his report in the mail but took it directly to the meeting with the Secretary of State to give to him in person. Before Henry Kissinger had even said a word, his adviser explained that he had done the absolute maximum and that he could not really do any better. Henry Kissinger then replied: *"OK, in that case, this time I'll read it"*.

It is undoubtedly a ploy that has to be used and abused, especially when drawing up the assessment of a meeting with a seller: only let him leave with the impression that *"he will have to do a lot better"*. If the seller only does a little bit better, he will have the impression of having won, while the buyer will in any case have obtained something without effort.

2.7 DIVIDE AND RULE

Highlighting a contradiction between the respective words of the opposing negotiators can test and even break their cohesion thereby putting them in a position of inferiority.

At a given moment, the view point of one of the participants will inevitably be slightly different from that of their colleagues. It is sufficient to point out this difference in an assertive even aggressive manner, presenting it as a fundamental discrepancy. The participants will then attempt to justify themselves and the negotiator can simply refute the justifications until dissensions appear.

You will immediately note that this type of trick or ploy is on the borderline of the rules of ethics, and should be used with a great deal of care.

2.8 PHYSICAL DISCOMFORT

Physical discomfort consists of placing the other parties in more difficult negotiating conditions than yourself.

The commonest tricks are undoubtedly:

- Bright light from the windows that dazzles the sellers and prevents them from seeing the reactions of the negotiators and ultimately tiring them more quickly. It is sufficient to prepare a seating plan of the face-to-face type, whereby the buyers sit with their backs to the window and the sellers facing the window. This tactic requires bright outside light, a condition not always guaranteed.
- A long wait which not only stresses but also tires the sellers before they even start negotiations by, for example, leaving them to wait at the reception, with preferably no seats available. When applying this approach, it is advisable for the "delayed" negotiator to frequently apologise to ensure the sellers do not decide to postpone the meeting too quickly.
- Abnormally low seats for the sellers with respect to those of the buyers, or even the presence of a slight platform, which gives the other parties an unconscious feeling of inferiority.
- No food or refreshments, driving the other party to draw discussions to a close more rapidly. In any case it will shorten the debates on minor points, and sometimes even on the more important points, particularly if kept for the end of the negotiation, i.e. application of the Pareto principle. This tactic is all the more effective if the person using it takes sustenance just prior to the meeting.
- Alcohol can have a hard impact during a negotiation. One of the great classics is to have lunch halfway through the meeting and preferably before tackling the more important issues. The lunch then usually includes alcoholic beverages, for example irresistible vintage wines and liqueurs.

2.9 GETTING OUT OF AN IMPASSE

When deadlock is reached on one of the points in the negotiation, the situation risks to degenerate if the parties stick to their positions. The best trick for moving on is to divert attention in order to change the subject and revert back to the deadlock issue at the end of the negotiation. The sellers will probably not feel duped but changing the subject under these circumstances might very well suit them.

Another anecdote illustrates this principle although probably romanticised, while accepting its authenticity. The chairman of a Belgian group, a great hunter, was known to use a simple but effective trick. When a negotiation reached stalemate, he would look absent-mindedly out of his office window, which overlooked a large park, and then exclaim: *"Hey, a rabbit, did you see the rabbit? Over there, near the bush!"*. People around the table immediately looked out of the window, some even pretending to have seen the rabbit and then the chairman spoke for a few minutes about the pleasures of hunting... before resuming the negotiation from another angle and returning to the initial problem at a later stage.

A variant of this technique, clearly less poetic, is of course the classic interruption to a meeting, of the type *"Would you like a coffee?"*, only to resume the discussion a few minutes later having taken the initiative to change the subject.

Part 4

THE 4C METHOD

Chapter 1

The model

In general, the objective of the seller is to reach an agreement by overcoming the objections of the buyer.

In order to convince the sellers to change their perspective to the benefit of the buyer, it is essential to change their environment and to influence the parameters they use to conduct their negotiation. The more skilful the buyer with the devices available in the negotiating tool box, the more favourable the final agreement will be for them.

1.1 THE NEED FOR A PRACTICAL APPROACH

The market is overflowing with books describing negotiating mechanisms, strategies, techniques, tools, tricks & ploys, however, having a well stocked toolbox does not suffice, knowing how to properly use the tools available to you is of paramount importance.

The method was developed in 2005 for educational purposes. Originally the idea was to go a step further than just teaching a set of negotiating tools and develop a very simple method on how to better use this toolbox. The method then entered the business world, going from an educational to a practical tool.

1.2 THE GENERAL MODEL

The 4C method is based on applying a simple and practical approach to a model that combines all of the negotiating mechanisms, strategies, techniques, tools, tricks & ploys:

Negotiation profiles:
Aggressive vs friendly
Dominating vs submissive
Analytical vs intuitive
Assertive vs manipulative

Steps:
Preparation
Introductions
Opening the talks
Starting positions
Studying the positions
Confrontation
Searching for an agreement
Recording the result
Follow-up

Negotiation styles:
Coercion
Intransigence
Manipulation
Express negotiation
Compromise
Collaboration

Tools:
Competitive offering
Seating plan
Relevant questioning
Empathy
Attack-defence spiral
Analysis of the cost price
Room for manœuvre
Arguments
Concession-compensation
Participants
Calling out of bounds
Breaking off negotiations

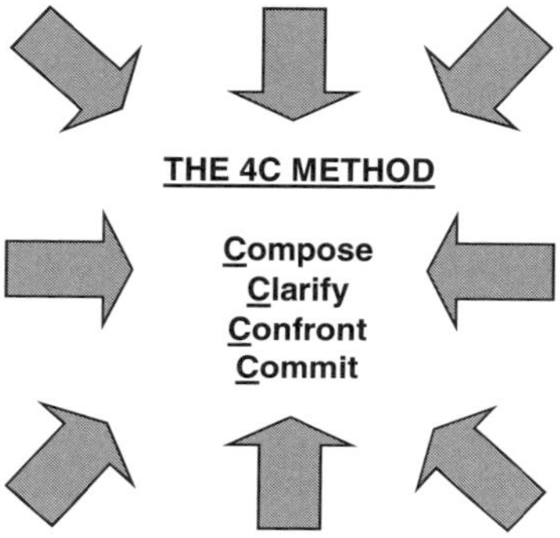

THE 4C METHOD

Compose
Clarify
Confront
Commit

Tricks & ploys:
Pareto principle
Never display enthusiasm
Never accept the first offer
Non-verbal behaviour
Always asks for the impossible
Do a lot better
Divide and rule
Physical discomfort
Getting out of an impasse

Procedural strategies:
Salami
Follow the flow
Give and take
Endurance

Decision strategies:
"Pull" & "Push"
4 steps
Application of force

Manipulative strategies:
Decoy
Underling
Good cop, bad cop
False pretext
Alliances

The 4C method is based on 4 attitudes that negotiators have to adopt during a negotiation, applying the most effective mechanisms, strategies and techniques in relation to the situation in which they find themselves: **C**ompose → **C**larify → **C**onfront → **C**ommit.

Each attitude meets a series of objectives to be achieved during each stage of the negotiation:

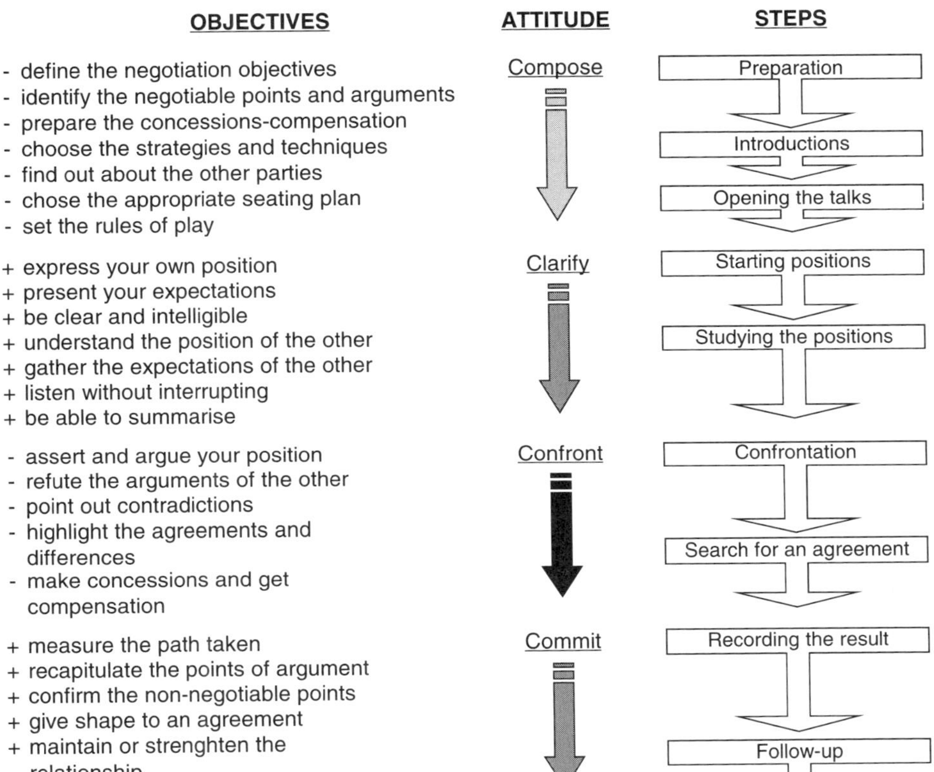

These 4 attitudes that the negotiator will adopt are defined as follows:

— Compose a negotiation plan and prepare for the talks on the basis of the parties concerned, the objectives of the negotiation, the negotiable points, the concessions-compensations, the most appropriate strategies and techniques, and the rules of play.

— Clarify your expectations to the other party, determine their exact position and measure the starting gap.

— Confront the other party's position by asserting and arguing your own position and by undermining or even refuting their position, so as to force them to hold nothing back and determine the real gap between the respective positions, before making concessions and propose solutions in order to finally bring the positions together.

— Commit to a deal and give shape to an agreement.

1.3 A GUARANTEED RESULT

The application of the 4C method guarantees a result at the end of the negotiation, whereas instinctive negotiation may end with an undetermined result, a sort of "not yes, not no", which neither displeases nor satisfies anybody. Having said that, the 4C method does not necessarily guarantee a positive outcome.

The final objective of a negotiation is of course, to reach an agreement that can be described as a:

— Consensus when each party has participated in the construction of the solution and they are unanimous with regard to the agreement. Adherence to it is then optimum.

— Compromise when the parties end up making successive adjustments with neither completely losing nor truly winning. It should be stressed that a compromise is regarded as worthless if the parties make concessions too quickly with neither party reaping any benefit.

— Concession when one of the parties has given up something without any real benefit or consideration.

In the absence of this, the parties still have a disagreement, that can be described as:

— Deferred when the parties believe they should meet again to give themselves another chance.

— Objective when the parties accept their differences without wanting to bridge them.

— Contradictory when the parties do not accept their respective positions.

In any case, it is good practice to summarise the starting and finishing positions to ensure that all parties are aware of their contributions towards the success or failure of the negotiation.

In this respect, follow-up is essential, irrespective of the outcome of the negotiation, for example:

— Send an e-mail, letter or memorandum to thank the parties and summarise the agreement and its implementation (e.g. a to do list).

— The same applies in the event of failure in order to 'freeze' the stumbling block and, if applicable, to start a new negotiation (e.g. proposed dates).

Chapter 2

The attitudes

To progress from a toolbox to a successful negotiation is a long road, comparable to the distance between theory and practice. The difficulty is to know what types of behaviours, styles, strategies, tools, tricks and ploys to use at what time and with what "mental" attitude.

2.1 THE "COMPOSE" ATTITUDE

The "compose" attitude is the recommended attitude for setting up the conditions of the negotiation: preparation, introductions and opening the talks.

It is a relatively neutral attitude towards the other party, as contacts are limited. It is thus neither aggressive nor friendly, neither dominating nor submissive. On the other hand, it becomes very analytical when pulling together the case file containing the objective and quantified elements of the supplier's offer, the cost price breakdown, competing offers, etc. It also has to be relatively manipulative during the preparation of the envisaged strategy and techniques.

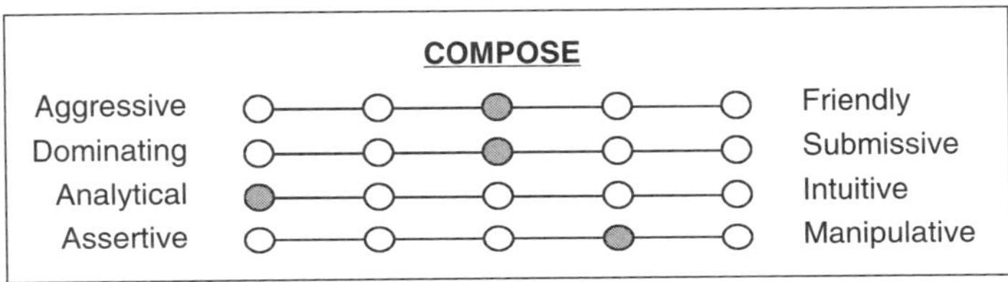

In this respect, it is an attitude that lends itself very well to the use of certain analytical tools during the preparation and certain more manipulative ones during the introductions and opening the talks:

COMPOSE

Tools	***Tricks & Ploys***
Competitive tendering	*Physical discomfort*
Analysis of the cost price	*Divide and rule*
Participants	
Seating plan	

When used, physical discomfort and dividing the adverse parties should be applied during the first exchanges.

2.2 THE "CLARIFY" ATTITUDE

The "clarify" attitude is the classic attitude to be adopted when presenting your positions and analysing the positions of the adverse party.

It is an attitude without emotion, not particularly friendly but on the other hand not aggressive. Furthermore, it is essential to listen without interruption during the respective presentations. An aggressive attitude could result in a reaction leading to an immediate confrontation on the viewpoints that have yet to be expressed or explained. On the other hand, the assertive attitude, or even the dominating attitude, helps to firmly establish the starting positions.

Finally, it is useful to be both analytical in the study of the items presented by the other party, and intuitive in the search for the more hidden components:

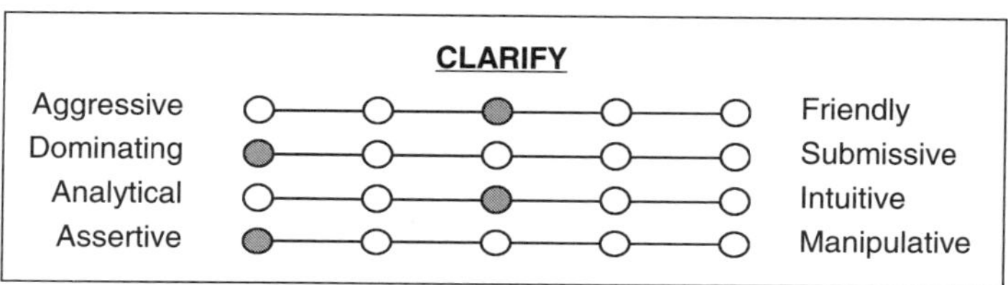

Relevant questioning is thus the most appropriate technique to precisely understand the position of the other person and to discover the hidden components, bearing in mind that an unacceptable position must be immediately disqualified:

CLARIFY

Tools	***Tricks & Ploys***
Relevant questioning	*Never display enthusiasm*
Calling out of bounds	*Never accept the first offer*
	Non-verbal behaviour

2.3 THE "CONFRONT" ATTITUDE

The "confront" attitude is an appropriate tactic during the confrontation phase and the search for an agreement phase.

It is a highly emotional attitude. The objective of the confrontation is to challenge the starting position of the other parties. The idea is to test its solidity and to get the other parties to move towards a more favourable position for yourself, and, more appropriately, to the seek an agreement.

The assertive and dominating attitudes are thus ideal, however, a certain aggressive approach could be anticipated, but without falling into the attack-defence spiral trap:

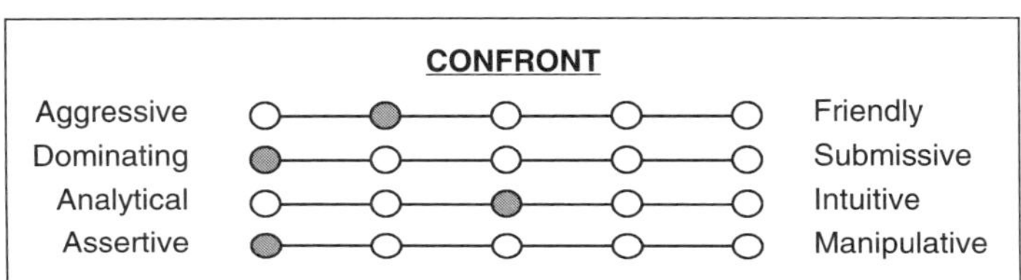

Given that the confrontation phase then evolves into the search for an agreement phase, aggression and domination gradually disappear to make way for the assertive attitude thus maintaining the positions subsequently acquired.

This attitude, which consists of provoking the other, requires the negotiators to have formerly defined their strategy during the preparation period. The first solution is to simply opt for one or more of the basic negotiating styles and to judiciously choose the style as the negotiation develops:

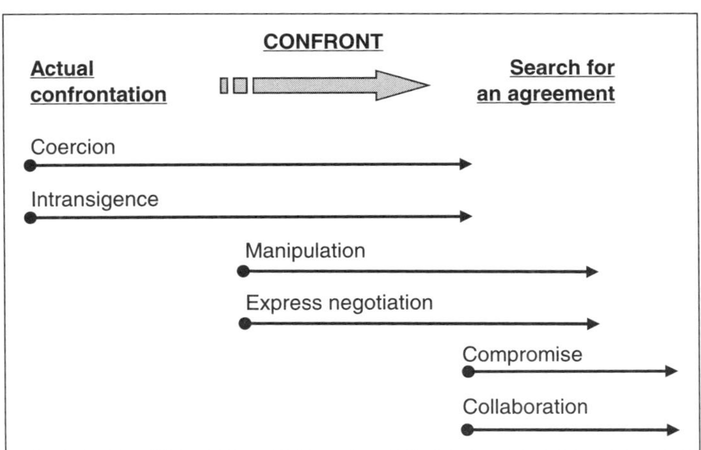

In fact, the more violent styles are more effective at the start of the confrontation when testing the adverse party. However, as the confrontation develops into the search for an agreement phase, the more important it becomes for the attitude to move towards the friendlier styles.

Another solution is to choose one or more of these strategies:

Procedural strategies:	**Decision strategies:**	**Manipulative strategies:**
Salami	"Pull" & "Push"	Decoy
Follow the flow	4 steps	Underlyng
Give and take	Application of force	Good cop, bad cop
Endurance		False pretext
		Alliances

With "confront" being the combat sport of negotiation, it is the attitude in which the greatest number of tools, tricks & ploys can be used:

CONFRONT	
Tools	***Tricks & Ploys***
Competitive tendering	*Pareto principle*
Arguments	*Always ask for the impossible*
Concession-compensation	*Do a lot better*
Room for manoeuvre	*Divide and rule*
Attack-defence spiral	*Getting out of an impasse*
Relevant questioning	*Non-verbal behaviour*
Calling out of bounds	
Breaking off negotiations	

Having said this, subtlety is often more effective than the heavy artillery approach during negotiations and it is advisable to avoid deploying all the tools, tricks and ploys that you know, at the risk of the adversary digging in their heels.

2.4 THE "COMMIT" ATTITUDE

The "commit" attitude is characterised by a state of mind conducive to calming the situation, being open to a deal and reaching an agreement. Even if no agreement is reached, continuing the confrontation would serve no purpose. Clearly, in such cases, it is more appropriate to calm the situation with a view to giving the parties a chance in a new negotiation.

This attitude is thus characterised by a subtle balance between friendliness and assertiveness to avoid revisiting the negotiation during the drawing up of the draft agreement. Moreover, it is important to be very analytical when drawing up the draft to ensure that it thoroughly reflects the will of the parties.

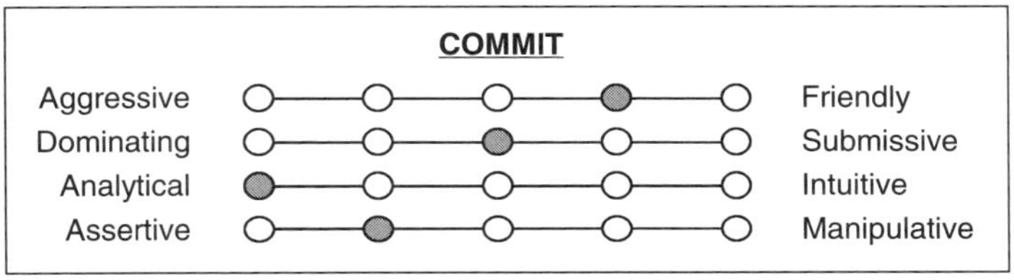

	COMMIT	
Aggressive	○—○—○—●—○	Friendly
Dominating	○—○—●—○—○	Submissive
Analytical	●—○—○—○—○	Intuitive
Assertive	○—●—○—○—○	Manipulative

Consequently, relevant questioning is largely used to ensure that all of the clauses of the draft are perfectly understood. Empathy enables restoring confidence and the relationship with the other parties, sometimes shaken by the preceding confrontation.

COMMIT

Tools	***Tricks & Ploys***
Empathy	*Pareto principle (Colombo effect)*
Relevant questioning	

The sole exception to this gentlemanly attitude is recourse to the Colombo effect whereby negotiations suddenly restart at a time when the other party least expects, or at a point when they do not necessarily want to resume the negotiation.

Part 5

CASE STUDY

Chapter 1

The case of GOS Logistics Plc

The objective of this case study is to put the 4C method into practice.

1.1 THE GROUPS

Three working groups should be created whose task consists of preparing for the negotiation, electing two representatives per group to take on the roles of the participants and finally participating in the negotiation meeting on 26th October.

To this end, the three groups have access to all sections of this chapter, unlike the sections of chapter 2 which are specific to each group and of a confidential nature.

1.2 THE SCENARIO

The GOS Logistics Plc case involves 3 groups of players:

- GOS (George & Oscar Scott) Logistics Plc: a British logistics services provider whose registered office and largest Distribution Centre are located in Birmingham.
- 4C Associates Ltd: an award winning consultancy and managed services firm with offices in London and Brussels, specialising in helping British and Continental European clients, like GOS Logistics Plc, achieve cost leadership.
- Atlantic Recruitment Ltd: a temping agency specialised in the recruitment of blue-collar workers in the logistics sector, located in Rugeley, North of Birmingham.

Rahul Patel has been the manager of the Birmingham Distribution Centre for 8 years. He was the person who negotiated the contract with Atlantic Recruitment, some three years ago, for the sourcing of temporary staff specialising in the field of warehousing. The contract with Atlantic Recruitment will be renewed on

1st January for 12 months, in the absence of a termination letter sent by registered post before 31 September, i.e. within the next 3 weeks. Rahul has just come out of the office of Jo Waggott, the HR Manager of GOS Logistics, with whom he has discussed the Atlantic Recruitment contract. He informed Jo that he was satisfied in general with the services provided by Atlantic Recruitment, although there had been a series of problems over the last 12 months: agency staff coming late or not turning up, and a drop in the productivity of certain agency staff during the end-of-year rush. Jo concluded that they would do well to bang their fists on the table.

Linda Seagrave, supply chain procurement expert at 4C Associates in London, has just been appointed Project Manager in charge of the GOS Logistics assignment. Her role is to harmonise the practices for purchases of commodities for all the sites and to reduce the TOC (Total Cost of Ownership). She has just completed, not without difficulty, the first phase of her assignment, i.e. the 3rd party spend analysis and the inventory of all contracts and their expiry dates. Her Outlook® has reminded her of the forthcoming expiry of the Birmingham agency staff contract. She picks up her phone and dials the number of Rahul Patel. Linda has only had contact with him by e-mail, when her Senior Analyst, Didi Todorova, of Bulgarian origin, carried out the inventory of the contracts. She said that with a bit of luck, the opportunity to make savings would make Rahul more cooperative than he had been in their initial contact. She recalls having had to wait 6 weeks for the information that Didi had requested. *"After all, perhaps it was just an accident"* she said to herself *"we will quickly know"*.

Peter Macleod, Manager of Atlantic Recruitment, was extremely surprised when he opened the registered letter that the receptionist had just given him. After three years of good and loyal service, GOS Logistics was ending their contract, without even a phone call, and was putting the contract out to competitive tender. And that was not all, the letter was not only signed by Rahul and Jo, with whom the relationship was excellent, but also by a certain Linda Seagrave from 4C Associates in London. Peter immediately called the commercial representative responsible for the account in order to analyse the user requirements, draw up a proposal and prepare for the meeting with GOS Logistics on 26th October. *"Dear me, as if we had nothing better to do"* Peter thought to himself.

1.3 THE REQUEST FOR QUOTATION

Claire Leroy came out of Peter Macleod's office and flopped heavily into her chair. *"What a pain"* she thought. It was the last thing that anybody at Atlantic Recruitment had been expecting. She immediately set to work. *"The Request for Quotation seems easy to get through, at least that's something"* she thought while beginning to read the document.

Customer

GOS Logistics Plc is a British company, providing 3rd party logistics services, with registered office and main site in Birmingham.

The company has a warehouse of 40,000 m² and 440 people and offers its B2B customers warehousing, handling and distribution services for their food products to the main supermarket chains of the country. GOS Logistics has just purchased 4 other distribution centres in Aberdeen, Liverpool, Manchester and Portsmouth, bringing the total to 140,000 m² and 1,400 people, with a consolidated turnover of £123 million.

Control

GOS Logistics Plc is a wholly owned subsidiary of a Scottish private investment company, RMS L.P. (Roberts, McGregor, Swire), based in Glasgow. Already present on the road transportation market, RMS has just made significant investments in logistics services with the acquisition of Brenner Am Rhein Logistiks GmbH in Germany, La Logistique des Alpes Sarl in France and GOS Logistics Plc in the United-Kingdon with now a consolidated turnover of £972 million.

Request for quotation

A quotation is requested for the provision of temporary labour specialising in logistics, for a duration of three years, as of next 1st January. The main functions are:

- Receiving operators (unloading & goods inspection).
- Forklift truck operators (put-away).
- Pickers (pick & pack).
- Loaders (loading of the vehicles).

In the first phase, only the Birmingham site will be subject to consultation for the following requirements:

- Around 16,500 days of temporary labour per year, each of 7 hours 30 minutes, i.e. 317 days per week on average.
- Broken down into 63 on Monday, 32 on Tuesday and Wednesday, 79 on Thursday, 63 on Friday, 32 on Saturday and 16 on Sunday.
- In the time slots of 06:00-13:30, 13:30-21:00 and 21:00-04:30.
- With the precise number of days and the distribution in the time slots being announced before midday the prior day.
- With permanent staff present between 05:45 and 21:15 to receive and direct the agency staff to their place of work, to respond promptly in the event of absence of one or more agency staff, and to receive the needs for the following day.
- With a performance indicator calculated in relation to the number of days totally worked divided by the number of days ordered the day before, accompanied by a penalty of 5% of the amount of the services for the day in the event of a result below 98.5%, plus an additional penalty of 1% for each 0.5% band below 98.5%.
- With the termination of the contract to the charge of the service provider in the event of performance below 98.5% for three consecutive days, or on average over the whole week from Monday to Sunday, with £140,000 as liquidated damages to compensate for starting up with a new service provider.

Response form

The bidders must submit their proposal in the following format:

Response form

The bidders must submit their proposal in the following format:

COST BREAKDOWN	VOLUME		AMOUNT	
Management team	**Quantity**	**Unit**	**£/Month**	**£/Year**
....	...	FTE	... £	... £
....	...	FTE	... £	... £
		s/total		... £
Agency staff	**Quantity**	**Unit**	**£/Month**	**£/Year**
Receiving operators	1.0	FTE	... £	
Forklift truck operators	1.0	FTE	... £	
Pickers	1.0	FTE	... £	
Loaders	1.0	FTE	... £	
		Average	... £	
		Hours	x 7.5	
		s/total	x 16,500 =	... £
Others	**Quantity**	**Unit**	**£/Month**	**£/Year**
....	...	...		... £
....	...	...		... £
		s/total		... £
TOTAL				... £

INVOICING	VOLUME		AMOUNT
Category	**Quantity**	**£**	**£/Year**
Fixed amount	12	...	... £
Variable amount	7.5 x 16,500	...	... £
TOTAL			... £

The proposal will be first presented in the offices of GOS Logistics in Birmingham on 26th October. The bidders will present their quotation and be informed of their competitiveness and, if applicable, the items to be revised.

Chapter 2

The role of the participants

Each group of participants has a precise role to play, of a confidential nature vis-à-vis the other groups, and with final objective the preparation of the meeting on 26th October during which they will negotiate the new service contract. May the best group win!

2.1 THE ROLE OF RAHUL AND JO (GROUP 1)

Rahul Patel hung up the phone to see the smile on the face of Jo Waggott seated opposite him, he thought to himself that he must have been right on target there. He had just congratulated Linda Seagrave for the splendid user requirements that he had received from her and which had been attached to the letter of termination which had been addressed to Atlantic Recruitment. *"You've got a nerve"* Jo said to him laughing. *"You do not seem overly irritated by the fact that a consultant is sticking her nose into our business"* added Jo leaving the office.

Rahul sighed as he really did have other things more important to do, for example to find a way to double his profit before tax for next year, an objective his boss had just set him... and, in addition, his bonus would depend on it. He again immersed himself into the forecasts that the finance department had just sent to all members of the Executive Committee.

He almost choked seeing the profit forecast by his Manchester counterpart, who continued to be at the helm. *"He will be bragging at the next Executive Committee meeting. It doesn't surprise me that my boss has asked me to double my profit. And then when are we going to stop paying for Aberdeen and Portsmouth"*, he sighed.

"How am I going to achieve this? Mmmh… What if 4C Associates would be part of the equation after all?", he thought.

GOS LOGISTICS IN '000 £	CC01 BIRMINGHAM	CC03 LIVERPOOL	CC04 ABERDEEN	CC05 MANCHESTER	CC06 PORTSMOUTH	GRAND TOTAL
Sales	38,570	30,881	16,685	25,421	11,596	123,153
Salaries	-22,337	-17,274	-9,378	-14,299	-6,399	-69,689
Agency staff	-2,143	-2,314	-1,736	-1,736	-1,157	-9,086
Other personnel expenses	-1,200	-921	-501	-750	-325	-3,697
Housing and facility	-5,301	-4,184	-2,272	-3,453	-1,537	-16,748
Leasing expenses	-2,269	-1,896	-1,430	-1,406	-935	-7,936
Other operating expenses	-2,809	-2,388	-1,791	-1,791	-1,194	-9,973
Operating margin	2,511	1,903	-422	1,987	47	6,026
Management fees	-1,929	-1,544	-834	-1,271	-580	-6,158
EBITDA	582	359	-1,257	716	-533	-132
Goodwill amortisation	0	0	0	0	0	0
Fixed asset depreciation	-174	-148	-111	-111	-74	-619
EBIT	408	211	-1,368	605	-607	-751

The ring of the telephone interrupted Rahul's thoughts. It was Jo. *"Have you read your e-mails? Didi Todorova has just sent us a comparison of the costs of Atlantic Recruitment and their benchmark, a certain Go-4-Temp. We will need to discuss it to decide on our strategy."* Rahul muttered a sort of "yes" and hung up.

Jo opened and read the spreadsheet from Didi. Jo immediately realised that the costs were significantly lower. *"Okay but if the quality of the temps and the reliability of the agency are not up to scratch, it will be a catastrophe. We will definitely have to keep control of the negotiating process"*, Jo thought.

Rahul read the spreadsheet with a smile. *"Okay, that gives me an idea"*, he thought and sent an Outlook® invitation to Jo for lunch time the next day with *"Subject : Tender preparation meeting"*.

On the next day, Rahul and Jo had just finished their sandwich when Jo exclaimed *"Deal. Let's see how we can down two birds with one stone: improve performance and cut cost, say ideally 5% but not less than 3% anyway"*. Rahul smiled and thought: *"Gosh. 5% on a spend of £2,143k with Atlantic Recruitment makes… errrr… £107k per annum! I would already be happy with 4%."* Rahul stood up, went to the white board and started to write their objectives with 4 columns labelled "Ideal Position", "Realistic Position", "Fallback Position" and "Arguments". Jo took a blank sheet of paper, started making a checklist while thinking *"Negotiation points, yes, but also, agenda, seating plan, breakdown of the new price, concessions-compensations, possibly some sort of decoy… Who will lead the meeting, by the way?"*, Jo said.

COST BREAKDOWN	GO-4-TEMP				ATLANTIC			
	VOLUME		AMOUNT		VOLUME		AMOUNT	
Management team	Quantity	Unit	£/Month	£/Year	Quantity	Unit	£/Month	£/Year
Administration	**2.0**	**FTE**	**2 ,950 £**	**70,800 £**	**0.0**	**FTE**	**- £**	**- £**
Replaceme	**0.2**	**FTE**	**- £**	**- £**	**0.0**	**FTE**	**- £**	**- £**
....	-	-	**- £**	**- £**	-	-	**- £**	**- £**
....	-	-	**- £**	**- £**	-	-	**- £**	**- £**
		s/total		70,800 £		s/total		- £
Agency staff	Quantity	Unit	£/Month	£/Year	Quantity	Unit	£/Month	£/Year
Receiving	**1.0**	**FTE**	**14.47 £**		**1.0**	**FTE**	**17.32 £**	
Forklift truck	**1.0**	**FTE**	**14.47 £**		**1.0**	**FTE**	**17.32 £**	
Pickers	**1.0**	**FTE**	**15.50 £**		**1.0**	**FTE**	**17.32 £**	
Loader	**1.0**	**FTE**	**14.47 £**		**1.0**	**FTE**	**17.32 £**	
		Average	14.70 £			Average	17.32 £	
		Hours	x 7.5			Hours	x 7.5	
		s/total	x 16,500 =	1,819,125 £		s/total	x 16,500 =	2,143,350 £
O hers	Quantity	Unit	£/Month	£/Year	Quantity	Unit	£/Month	£/Year
Agency	**8**	**%**		**151,194 £**	-	-		**- £**
....	-	-		**- £**	-	-		**- £**
....	-	-		**- £**	-	-		**- £**
			s/total	151,194 £			s/total	- £
TOTAL				2,041,119 £				2,143,350 £
INVOICING	**VOLUME**		**AMOUNT**		**VOLUME**		**AMOUNT**	
Category	Quantity	£		£/Year	Quantity	£		£/Year
Fixed	**12**	**18,500 £**		**221,994 £**	**12**	**- £**		**- £**
Variable	**7.5 x 16,500**	**14.70 £**		**1,819,125 £**	**7.5 x 16,500**	**17.32 £**		**2,143,350 £**
TOTAL				2,041,119 £				2,143,350 £
CROSS-	COMPETITOR		%	£/Year	COMPETITOR		%	£/Year
Differenc	**Versus ATLANTIC**		**-4.8%**	**- 102,231 £**	**Versus**	**GO-4-**	**+ 5.0%**	**102,231 £**

2.2 THE ROLE OF LINDA AND DIMITRINA (GROUP 2)

Dimitrina Todorova took an assured step into Linda Seagrave's office. The comparison of the respective costs of Go-4-Temp and Atlantic Recruitment made no doubt that the latter party would not be able to stay the race.

It has to be said that the prices of Go-4-Temp had been argued over fiercely by 4C Associates. Having said that, a flicker of a smile appeared on Didi's face when thinking back to the negotiating session during which Linda had played the role of bad cop and Didi the good cop. *"The boss of Go-4-Temp and his sales director emerged from the meeting truly exhausted"*.

"You seem to be in a good mood" exclaimed Linda. Didi reminded her of the famous negotiating session. Linda smiled and replied that the negotiation had been especially well-prepared and that she and Didi had used the 4C method to the full extend to achieve their aspirations.

Didi presented the results of her comparison between Go-4-Temp and Atlantic Recruitment. *"Not only is Atlantic Recruitment around £100,000 more expensive, but their pricing also lacks the most elementary transparency"* commented Didi before concluding *"I propose pushing the Birmingham site towards Go-4-Temp and wait for the expiry of the contract at the other sites to convert all of GOS Logistics and therefore make 5% annual and sustainable savings"*.

Linda's face took on a doubtful expression. No doubt she saw the value of Go-4-Temp gaining ground: reducing costs, increasing volume with them and the possibility to revise the price downwards, fewer service providers to manage, etc. in particular as she had the responsibility to reduce the TOC by 5% over 12 months, nevertheless she wondered how far Atlantic Recruitment could go if they were cornered.

"For the moment you're right, Didi, but let's leave the negotiation process to take its course, and see the outcome", Linda replied. She thought of the request for quotation that Atlantic Recruitment currently had to work on and asked Didi to prepare a battle plan for the meeting on 26th October with ideal, realistic and fall-back positions and arguments for each of their objectives as well as an agenda for the meeting. She stressed the choice of a strategy and the possible role plays with the Birmingham team.

"Make me a full proposal with negotiation points including idealistic, realistic and fallback positions and arguments, seating plan, participant role descriptions, breakdown of the new price, concessions-compensations, processing, decision and manipulative strategies and so on", she said. *"We will review all of this together"*.

Linda had always been of the opinion that building a battle plan is to take de facto control of the operations. *"I believe 4% is realistic and 5% is quiet idealistic but why not give it a try. Still, don't forget our commitment to GOS Logistics is to reduce temping agency costs by 3%, possibly more", she added.*

COST BREAKDOWN	GO-4-TEMP				ATLANTIC RECRUITMENT			
	VOLUME		AMOUNT		VOLUME		AMOUNT	
Management team	**Quantity**	**Unit**	**£/Month**	**£/Year**	**Quantity**	**Unit**	**£/Month**	**£/Year**
Administration coordinator	2.0	FTE	2 ,950 £	70,800 £	0.0	FTE	- £	- £
Replacement	0.2	FTE	- £	- £	0.0	FTE	- £	- £
....	-	-	- £	- £	-	-	- £	- £
....	-	-	- £	- £	-	-	- £	- £
		s/total		**70,800 £**		**s/total**		**- £**
Agency staff	**Quantity**	**Unit**	**£/Month**	**£/Year**	**Quantity**	**Unit**	**£/Month**	**£/Year**
Receiving operators	1.0	FTE	14.47 £		1.0	FTE	17.32 £	
Forklift truck operators	1.0	FTE	14.47 £		1.0	FTE	17.32 £	
Pickers	1.0	FTE	15.50 £		1.0	FTE	17.32 £	
Loaders	1.0	FTE	14.47 £		1.0	FTE	17.32 £	
		Average	**14.70 £**			**Average**	**17.32 £**	
		Hours	**x 7.5**			**Hours**	**x 7.5**	
		s/total	**x 16,500 =**	**1,819,125 £**		**s/total**	**x 16,500 =**	**2,143,350 £**
Others	**Quantity**	**Unit**	**£/Month**	**£/Year**	**Quantity**	**Unit**	**£/Month**	**£/Year**
Agency commission	8	%		151,194 £	-	-		- £
....	-	-		- £	-	-		- £
....	-	-		- £	-	-		- £
			s/total	151,194 £			s/total	- £
TOTAL				**2,041,119 £**				**2,143,350 £**
INVOICING	**VOLUME**		**AMOUNT**		**VOLUME**		**AMOUNT**	
Category	**Quantity**	**£**		**£/Year**	**Quantity**	**£**		**£/Year**
Fixed amount	12	18,500 £		221,994 £	12	- £		- £
Variable amount	7.5 x 16,500	14.70 £		1,819,125 £	7.5 x 16,500	17.32 £		2,143,350 £
TOTAL				**2,041,119 £**				**2,143,350 £**
CROSS-	**COMPETITOR**		**%**	**£/Year**	**COMPETITOR**		**%**	**£/Year**
Differenc	Versus ATLANTIC RECRUITMENT		-4.8%	- 102,231 £	Versus	GO-4-TEMP	+ 5.0%	102,231 £

When Didi left the office, Linda smiled as she had just thought of an idea. At the meeting with both suppliers she would ask them for an up-front payment of £50,000 to demonstrate their eagerness to work with GOS Logistics for 3 years. *"In any event"*, she said to herself, *"it will unsettle them and we will then see what evolves."*

2.3 THE ROLE OF PETER AND CLAIRE (GROUP 3)

Peter opened the Excel® file that Claire had sent him containing the profit and loss account of GOS Logistics:

P&L in '000 £ (GOS Logistics)	YTD Sep	Forecast Q4	Total
Days of temporary labor	11,688	4,813	16,500
Rate	17.32 £	17.32 £	17.32 £
Sales	1,518 £	625 £	2,143 £
Salaries - blue-collars	**- 1,278 £**	**- 526 £**	**- 1,804 £**
Salaries - white-collars	- 71 £	- 21 £	- 92 £
Operating margin	**170 £**	**78 £**	**247 £**
	11.2%	12.4%	11.5%

Peter was angry at having to compete on his most profitable contract. Not only was the operating margin very positive, covering for general & administration, depreciation and exceptional expenses but, above all, it was high enough for Peter not to be too concerned about certain other less profitable contracts.

When Claire came into Peter's office she immediately exploded: *"Have you seen what they're asking us to do? They're asking us to itemise our cost prices... and... and that will clearly show our 5% additional hidden margin!"*. Peter had been expecting something like this from a cost leadership consultancy firm like 4C Associates and sank back into his armchair thinking. He then calmed down his commercial representative and asked her to present the work that she had prepared.

Claire said that she had presented the current tender in the format desired by 4C Associates, without changing the commercial conditions, but admitted to her helplessness in the face of the transparency brought about by the format to be followed.

Vexed, Claire added that she did not have a great deal of choice, either she clearly showed the margin or she left it out and then the total cost price would not correspond to the total invoicing. *"That would be taking them for idiots. They would quickly see the difference between the two and determine the margin for themselves"* Peter retorted. In addition, Peter thought to himself that it would give GOS Logistics an argument to reproach them for not playing the game.

Peter explained that they would have to play it smart as there would certainly be competitors around and a concession on the price was inevitable. The amount and form still had to be determined.

COST BREAKDOWN	ATLANTIC RECRUITMENT (QUOTATION)			
	VOLUME		AMOUNT	
Management team	**Quantity**	**Unit**	**£/Month**	**£/Year**
Administration coordinator	2.5	ETP	2,844 £	85,322 £
Replacement	0.2	ETP	2,844	£ 6,826 £
....	-	-	- £	- £
....	-	-	- £	- £
		s/total		**92,148 £**
Agency staff	**Quantity**	**Unit**	**£/Month**	**£/Year**
Receiving operators	1.0	ETP	14.57 £	
Forklift truck operators	1.0	ETP	14.13 £	
Pickers	1.0	ETP	15.40 £	
Loaders	1.0	ETP	14.22 £	
		Average	**14.58 £**	
		Hours	**x 7.5**	
		s/total	**x 16,500 =**	**1,804,275 £**
Others	**Quantity**	**Unit**	**£/Month**	**£/Year**
Agency commission	8.0	%		1 51,714 £
Additional margin				95,213 £
....	-	-		- £
		s/total		**246,927 £**
TOTAL				**2,143,349.72 £**

INVOICING	VOLUME		AMOUNT
Category	**Quantity**	**£**	**£/Year**
Fixed amount	12	- £	- £
Variable amount	7.5 x 16,500	17.32 £	2,143,350 £
TOTAL			**2,143,350.00 £**

Claire was also worried about the announcement made to the media that same morning concerning the acquisition of Atlantic Recruitment by Temp*Expert*, a US group based in Minneapolis (MN), who made several acquisitions in Europe over the last few years. She was aware of their strong presence in France and Germany and all the interest in their investment in a British agency, however, she wondered whether this change of control might not scare GOS Logistics.

"Indeed, let's have a lunch and finalise a strategy for our new meeting" replied Peter. *"I cannot afford to lose GOS Logistics so I am ready to give 4% away but not more"*, he added. Looking at Claire's gloomy face, Peter explained that 4% had to be a fallback position. Walking to the door, he took her by the shoulders and said *"What about proposing 2% to start with, huh?"* Claire smiled and said *"open with an idealistic 2% reduction, stick to a more realistic 3% as long as possible so as to keep away from the dangerous 4% fallback position. I see where you are coming from"*. She concluded they had better get well prepared, with negotiation points with idealistic, realistic and fallback positions and arguments as well

as agenda, participant role descriptions, breakdown of the new price, concessions-compensations and all. *"Yes! And why not take them by surprise also?"* said Peter. *"The best form of defence is attack. So let's leverage the power of TempExpert to propose our services to GOS other distribution centres…"*, he added.

Glossary

4C method: reasoned negotiating method based on four mental attitudes that enable the negotiatingtool box to be systematically applied. The attitudes are "**C**ompose", "**C**larify", "**C**onfront" and "**C**ommit".

4 steps: decision strategy that consists of inciting the other party to eventually adopt a position that he will judge favourably, while in reality it will only be one better than the one he wanted to avoid.

Aggressive (profile): natural behaviour by which a negotiator looks for a win-lose result through a conflicting relationship as he can only concede to having won his negotiation if the other party has lost.

Alliance: manipulative strategy that consists of contacting another potential "ally" in the negotiation with a view to joining forces, officially or unofficially, and taking turns in the arguments.

Analytical (profile): natural behaviour by which negotiators follow a sequential and progressive process which leads them to analyse the decision.

Application of force: decision strategy that consists of forcing the hand of the other party, being the strongest, asserting yourself and your position.

Argument: negotiating tool that consists of distilling the most relevant, specific, objective, original and concise arguments during the talks, in order to counteract the arguments of the other parties and possibly influence them to obtain concessions.

Assertive (profile): natural behaviour by which a negotiator openly seeks their ultimate goal by clearly asserting and adopting his positions.

Attack-defence spiral (avoidance of the): negotiating tool that consists of avoiding counterattacking in the event of attack, and recognising the difference between the problems and the people.

Breaking off negotiations: negotiating tool that consists of breaking off the dialogue in order to put enormous pressure on the other person for whom there is nothing left to do but make an additional concession to restore the dialogue, or to take responsibility for the failure of the negotiation.

Calling out of bounds: negotiating tool that consists of sanctioning the behaviour of a party who goes beyond the bounds of acceptability vis-à-vis the other party, and against common morals, laws and regulations, business ethics or the respect of people.

Clarify: assertive and dominating mental attitude advocated by the 4C method when clarifying your own position and analysing the positions of the other party.

Coercion (negotiation based on): natural negotiation style that relies on the willpower that one person imposes on the other.

Collaboration (negotiation based on): natural negotiation style that relies on the principle of negotiating the respective objectives openly and finding a solution together that meets the majority if not all of the objectives.

Colombo (effect): trick & ploy in a negotiation, which consists of raising a last stumbling block by making a last demand, just before an agreement is reached in an attempt to obtain a final concession.

Commit: analytical and reasonably assertive attitude that is recommended by the 4C method when formalising the agreement.

Competitive tendering: negotiating tool that consists of making rival sellers compete with one another to the benefit of the buyer.

Compose: relatively neutral mental attitude in the relationship with the other party; highly analytical as advocated by the 4C method when setting up the conditions for the negotiation: preparation, introductions and opening of the dialogue.

Compromise (negotiation based on): natural negotiation style that relies on the principle of mutual concessions.

Concession-compensation (matrix of): negotiating tool that consists of identifying, during the preparation for the negotiation, the compensation that you will endeavour to get from the other party for each concession requested by them.

Confront: assertive and dominating mental attitude, even slightly aggressive, advocated by the 4C method during the confrontation of the starting positions and the search for an agreement.

Confrontation: a stage in the negotiation process which consists of breaking the artificial equilibrium between the parties and their positions in order to find a new more representative balance between the opposing parties.

Good cop, bad cop: manipulative strategy that consists of creating complicity with the other party, taking their side in order to better influence them.

Cost price analysis: negotiating tool that consists of not being satisfied with just a total price, but asking for a comprehensive breakdown in order to increase the discussion points and arguments.

Decision strategy: strategy applied in a negotiation to influence the decision-making process of the other person in order to obtain a faster and more favourable decision rather than follow the path of their own normal decision-making process.

Decoy: manipulative strategy that consists of making the other party believe that a point of the negotiation is crucial, with an unacceptable demand, when it is in fact secondary. The person who employs this strategy will subsequently abandon all ambitions in this respect, but it ensures a good payback.

Divide and rule: trick & ploy in a negotiation that consists of highlighting a contradiction between the respective words of the opposing negotiators, in order to test and even break their cohesion, thereby putting them in a position of inferiority.

Dominating (profile): natural behaviour by which a negotiator deliberately seeks to establish an unbalanced relationship in their favour and to direct the negotiation in their favour.

Empathy: negotiating tool that consists of immersing oneself in the subjective world of the other person and understanding their logic.

Endurance: procedural strategy that consists of playing on time and prolonging the negotiation.

Enthusiasm (never display): trick & ploy in a negotiation that consists of systematically displaying scepticism, a lack of enthusiasm, indecision and preference for a competitor in order to incite the other party to surpass themselves and "hold nothing back".

Express negotiation: natural negotiation style that relies on the ability of a negotiator to prevent the other party from putting forward their point of view and driving them to accept a proposal.

False pretext: manipulative strategy that puts pressure on the conditions that you want to obtain from the supplier (e.g. the price) or on the negotiation procedure (e.g. timing) in order to obtain one or more concessions.

First offer (never accept the): trick & ploy in a negotiation that consists of systematically rejecting the first offer, even if it is attractive, in order to force a negotiation and to avoid too rapid an agreement causing the other party to retract at a later stage.

Follow the flow: procedural strategy that consists of negotiating the various points in the order set out in the draft document which is being used as the basis for the negotiation.

Follow-up: step in the negotiation process that consists of implementing the agreement or subsequently resuming the negotiation in the event of failure.

Friendly (profile): natural behaviour by which a negotiator seeks to establish a climate of trust with the other person through a certain social proximity and complicity.

Give and take: procedural strategy that consists of grouping the items to be negotiated and the reciprocal concessions into balanced "packages".

Intuitive (profile): natural behaviour by which a negotiator proceeds emotionally by perceiving the components of talks before the decision suddenly crystallises.

Intransigence (negotiation based on): natural stereotypical negotiation based on the refusal of a party to make any concessions.

Introductions: step in the negotiation process that consists of stating the name, position, level of authority and, if applicable, the role of each party in the negotiation process.

Impasse (getting out of an): trick & ploy in a negotiation which consists of diverting attention if deadlock is reached and the parties stick to their positions by changing the subject and reverting back to the contentious issue at the end of the negotiation.

Impossible (always ask for the): trick & ploy in a negotiation that consists of actually asking for the impossible based on the principle that, although excessive, the demand may sometimes tally with what the other party is prepared to give up and also because it gives greater room for manoeuvre in the subsequent negotiation.

Lose-lose (result): outcome of a negotiation process by which the parties have neutralised each other to the extent that neither has achieved the desired result. It is often the outcome of a failed "take it or leave it" tactic.

Manipulation (negotiation based on): natural negotiation style that relies on deception.

Manipulative (profile): natural behaviour by which a negotiator continually acts covertly, never revealing their true intentions, with the objective of obtaining a win-lose result.

Manipulative strategy: strategy applied in a negotiation to influence the decision-making process of the other party by using concealment or stratagems to take advantage of them and to lead them, without their knowledge, to a solution they would not have otherwise chosen.

Must do a lot better: trick & ploy in a negotiation that enables the buyer, once the seller has announced the price, to immediately return the ball to the other court and compels the seller to justify the price and in many cases to make a concession.

Natural behaviour (profile): the natural tendency of negotiators towards a certain type of behaviour called negotiation profile which depends on their personality and their approach to negotiations.

Natural negotiation (style): natural and practically instinctive inclination of a negotiator towards a negotiating style which depends on their negotiation profile and the circumstances in which they find themselves.

Negotiating tool: effective negotiating technique, widely acknowledged and intended to challenge the starting position of the other party with a view to inciting them to revise their position.

Negotiation: process by which two or more parties manoeuvre and make concessions with respect to their starting positions, which are necessarily different, in order to bring their points of view together and reach an agreement.

Non-verbal behaviour: trick & ploy in a negotiation, which consists of taking advantage of non-verbal behaviour, such as exhaling audibly when the price is announced, adopting a surprised expression, shaking your head, rubbing your forehead in order to influence the other party in your favour.

Opening the dialogue: step in the negotiation process that consists of immediately defining the terms of reference of the negotiation and ensuring that the parties are on the same wavelength.

Pareto (principle): trick & ploy in a negotiation that consists of taking advantage of the fact that 80% of concessions are made in the last 20% of the negotiating time and by taking advantage of the approaching conclusion to raise problems hostile to the agreement.

Participants (choice of): a negotiating tool that consists of choosing, prior to the negotiations, the participants who will speak at a given moment in order to increase the impact of the dialogue.

Physical discomfort (taking advantage of): trick & ploy in a negotiation that consists of placing the other parties in more difficult negotiation conditions than yourself.

Preparation: step in the negotiation process that consists of putting together the case file containing the objective and quantified elements, and the plan for the dialogue.

Procedural strategy: strategy applied in negotiations to influence the order of the discussions and to lead them in a favourable direction for one or the other party.

Push and Pull: decision strategy that consists of alternately pushing and pulling the other party in order to force them to make one or more concessions earlier than they would have otherwise accepted.

Recording the result: a step in the negotiation process which consists of formally recording the fact of having reached an agreement or continuing disagreement by giving everybody the time to consider the situation before accepting the result.

Relevant questioning: negotiating tool that consists of asking a question not only to obtain the desired information, but also to adapt the method of communication to the phase that the negotiation is in.

Room for manoeuvre: negotiating tool that consists of making demands that are greater than reality, in order to create the possibility to reduce the demands in exchange for compensation from the other party.

Salami: procedural strategy that consists of cutting the negotiation into sections and negotiating the different sections successively.

Search for an agreement: step in the negotiation process that consists of bringing the different points of view together by making alternative proposals and counterproposals and by accepting concessions and obtaining compensation.

Seating plan: negotiating tool that consists of seating the parties so as to strengthen the strategy chosen to conduct the dialogue.

Starting position: step in the negotiation process that consists of each party setting out their starting position.

Study of the positions: step in the negotiation process that consists of each party analysing the position of the other.

Submissive (profile): natural behaviour by which a negotiator displays eludes of confrontation with the other and flees from the situation.

Trick and ploy in a negotiation: negotiating technique which is not scientific but highly dependent on the personality and the feeling of the negotiator adopting it.

Underling: manipulative strategy that consists of making the other person wrongly believe that you are not the real decision-maker in order to better manipulate them. This strategy is also called the fall guy technique.

Win-lose (result): outcome of a negotiation process by which one party obtains a substantial share of the result initially targeted, whereas the other party obtains very little.

Win-win (result): outcome of a negotiation process by which each party obtains the same share of the result initially targeted.

Bibliography

AUDEBERT (P), *Négocier pour la première fois*, Editions d'Organisation, 2005

AVRUCH (K), *Culture and Conflict Resolution*, United States Institute of Peace for Press, 1998

BELLENGER (L), *Les Fondamentaux de la négociation – Stratégies et tactiques gagnantes*, ESF Editeur, 2004

BERCOFF (M), *L'art de négocier – L'approche de Harvard en 10 questions*, Editions d'Organisation, 2005

BRETT (J) & GELFAND (M), *The Handbook of Negotiation and Culture*, Stanford University Press, 2004

BRETON (Ph), *Argumenter en situation difficile*, Pocket Evolution, 2006

BRODOW (E), *Negotiation Boot Camp: How to Resolve Conflict, Satisfy Customers, and Make Better Deals*, Broadway Business Published, 2006

CAMP (J), *Start with NO... The Negotiating Tools that the Pros Don't Want You to Know*, Crown Business, 2002

COHEN (R), *Negotiating Across Cultures: International Communication in an Interdependent World (Cross-Cultural Negotiation Books)*, United States Institute of Peace Press, 1998

DAWSON (R), *Secrets Of Power Negotiating : 15th Anniversay Edition Inside Secrets From a Master Negotiator*, Career Press, 2010

DELAHAYE (M), *La Négociation d'Affaires – Règles, Pratiques et Applications*, Dunod, 2005

DIGNALL (C), *Negotiation Skills in 7 Simple Steps*, Collins, 2014

FALCAO (H), *Value Negotiation: How to Finally Get the Win-Win Right*, Pearson, 2010

FISHER (R) & URY (W), *Getting to Yes: Negotiating a Agreement without Giving In*, Random House, 2012

GATES (S), *The Negotiation Book: Your Definitive Guide to Successful Negotiating*, John Wiley & Sons, 2010

HORTON (S), *Negotiation Mastery: Tools for the 21st Century Negotiator*, MX Publishing, 2012

JACKMAN (A), *How to Negotiate*, Hamlyn, 2004

LANGDON (K), *Succeed at Negotiating*, Dorling Kindersley, 2006

LEVINE (S), *The Book of Agreement: 10 Essential Elements for Getting the Results You Want*, Berrett-Koehler, 2002

LEWICKI (R), BARRY (B) & SAUNDERS (D), *Essentials of Negotiation*, McGraw-Hill, 2010

LEWICKI (R), *Negotiation*, McGraw-Hill, 2014

MALHOTRA (D), *Negotiation Genius: How to Overcome Obstacles and Achieve Brilliant Results at the Bargaining Table and Beyond*, Bantam Books, 2012

MENKEL-MEADOW (C), *What's Fair: Ethics for Negotiators*, Jossey-Bass, 2004

MOAL-ULVOAS (G), *Business Negotiation*, De Boeck, 2014

NOYE (D), *Gérer les conflits*, INSEP Consulting Editions, 2006

O'BRIEN (J), *Negotiation for Purchasing Professionals*, Kogan Page, 2013

PEELING (N), *Brilliant Negotiations: What the Best Negotiators Know, Do and Say*, Prentice Hall, 2010

PINET (A), *Secrets Of Power Negotiating: 15th Anniversay Edition Inside Secrets From a Master Negotiator*, Adams Media Corporation, 2011

POULET (O), *Savoir négocier ses contrats*, Damas, 2006

POWELL (M), *International Negotiations Student's Book*, Cambridge, 2012

RAIFFA (H), *The Art and Science of Negotiation*, Harvard University Press, 1990

REARDON (K), *The Skilled Negotiator: Mastering the Language of Engagement*, Jossey-Bass, 2004

RICH (C), *The Yes Book: The Art of Better Negotiation*, Virgin Books, 2013

ROMAIN (C), *Bien négocier*, Marabout Pratique, 2007

RONDOT (A), *Négocier avec la Process Com*, Dunod, 2006

SALACUSE (J), *The Global Negotiator – Making, Managing, and Mending the World in the Twenty-first Century*, Palgrave Macmillan, 2003

STARKEY (B), *International Negotiation in a Complex World*, Rowman & Littlefield Publishers, 2010

SUSSMANN (F) & BERCOFF (M), *Guide du négociateur d'affaires*, Editions d'Organisation, 2006

THOMPSON (L), *The Heart and Mind of the Negotiator*, Prentice Hall Business Publishing, 2001

WATKINS (M), *Breakthrough Business Negotiation: A Toolbox for Managers*, Jossey Bass, 2002

WATKINS (M), *Harvard Business Essentials – Negotiation*, Client Distribution Services, 2006

WHEELER (M), *The Art of Negotiation: How to Improvise Agreement in a Chaotic World*, Simon Schuster, 2013

WEZOWSKI (K) & WEZOWSKI (P), *The Micro Expressions Book for Business: How to read facial expressions for more effective negotiations, sales and recruitment*, New Vision, 2012

ZARTMAN (I) & RUBIN (J), *Power and Negotiation*, The University of Michigan Press, 2000

Filmography

DONALSON (R), *Thirteen Days,* based on the book by Ernest May and Philip Zelikow, with Kevin Costner, 2000
October 1962. An American spy plane discovers Soviet nuclear missiles on Cuban territory. If fired at the United States, they could wipe many American cities off the map. The trial of strength commences between the two superpowers. For John Fitzgerald Kennedy, the president of the United States, the threat is imminent. At his side are two of his most trusted men: Robert, his brother, and Kenneth O'Donnell, the chief of staff. For thirteen days the three men are at the centre of the most incredible and most dangerous negotiations where nothing more and nothing less than nuclear war was at stake.
A confrontation as amazing as it is historic which shows the strategies, techniques, tricks & ploys of negotiators who have to make terrible decisions for the future of humanity... leaving no margin for error.

LUMET (S), *Twelve Angry Men,* based on a play by Reginald Rose, with Henry Fonda, 1957
United States. The trial of a young man accused of murdering his father and where all evidence points to him. The district attorney develops a powerful and persuasive argument to prove his guilt, despite certain grey areas. When the jury retires to deliberate, eleven of the jurors are already convinced of the young man's guilt and only the twelfth juror has doubts. Alone against the others, he convinces, one by one, the remaining eleven jurors to find him not guilty.
An exceptional lesson in argument and persuasion, which has more to do with negotiating techniques than with justice as such.

MILLER (C), *Garde à Vue (Under Suspicion)*, based on a novel by John Wainwright, with Lino Ventura and Michel Serrault, 1981
New Year's Eve in a small town in Provence where the population is preoccupied by the rape and murder of two young girls. A lawyer, apparently with no history, is taken into police custody by the police chief who is convinced he has got his hands on the paedophile he is looking for. He attempts to extract a confession from the lawyer.

A surprising face-to-face confrontation between two characters that brings out the avoidance strategies of the two men. They turn around one another, size each other up, side-step, and even sometimes turn their backs on one another.

MOLINARO (E), *Le Souper* (*The Supper)*, based on a play by Jean-Claude Brisville, with Claude Brasseur and Claude Rich, 1992
June 1815. After having defeated Blucher in Ligny two days earlier, Napoleon loses the battle of Waterloo against all expectations. Paris is occupied by Austrian and Hungarian troops, while the British Navy is blockading the port of La Rochelle where Napoleon surrendered after having abdicated. In Paris, Talleyrand invites Fouché to dinner to negotiate the return of the Bourbon monarchy.
An example of subtle but ruthless negotiation between two men of formidable skill. The film is mainly about the confrontation phase in which the opposing parties vie with one another, using negotiating tools with subtlety and cynicism.